FORERUNNERS OF DANTE

FORERUNNERS OF DANTE

AN ACCOUNT OF SOME OF THE MORE
IMPORTANT VISIONS OF THE UNSEEN
WORLD, FROM THE EARLIEST TIMES

BY

MARCUS DODS
M.A. (EDIN.), B.A. (CANTAB.)

IMPORTED BY
CHARLES SCRIBNER'S SONS
NEW YORK

Printed by
MORRISON & GIBB LIMITED,
FOR
T. & T. CLARK, EDINBURGH.
LONDON: SIMPKIN, MARSHALL, HAMILTON, KENT, AND CO. LIMITED.
NEW YORK: CHARLES SCRIBNER'S SONS.

"*And is it likely that the soul, which is invisible, in passing to the place of the true Hades, which like her is invisible, and pure, and noble, and on her way to the good and wise God, whither, if God will, my soul is also soon to go,—that the soul, I repeat, if this be her nature and origin, will be blown away and destroyed immediately on quitting the body, as the many say? That can never be* . . .

But then, O my friends, he said, if the soul is really immortal, what care should be taken of her, not only in respect of the portion of time which is called life, but of eternity! And the danger of neglecting her from this point of view does indeed appear to be awful. If death had only been the end of all, the wicked would have had a good bargain in dying, for they would have been happily quit not only of their body, but of their own evil together with their souls. But now, inasmuch as the soul is manifestly immortal, there is no release or salvation from evil except the attainment of the highest virtue and wisdom. For the soul when on her progress to the world below takes nothing with her but nurture and education; and these are said greatly to benefit or greatly to injure the departed, at the very beginning of his journey thither."

SOCRATES, in the *Phædo* (Jowett).

CONTENTS.

	PAGE
INTRODUCTION	1

CHAPTER I.

BABYLONIAN AND EGYPTIAN LITERATURE.

Gilgamesh: Ea-bani—Ishtar—Minor Legends—Setme . 8

CHAPTER II.

GREEK AND ROMAN LITERATURE OF THE CLASSICAL PERIOD.

Odysseus—Pythagoras—Er—Scipio Africanus the Younger—Æneas—Minor References (The "Culex")—Thespesius—Timarchus—Parodies: The "Frogs," The "Menippus" . 28

CHAPTER III.

THE "DESCENSUS CHRISTI."

1 Peter iii. 18-20; iv. 6—Ephesians iv. 19—The Ethiopic Book of Enoch—The Ascension of Isaiah—The Gospel of Peter—The Gospel of Nicodemus—The Anaphora Pilati—Cædmon—The Harrowing of Hell (a Miracle-play) 83

CONTENTS

CHAPTER IV.

APOCRYPHAL LITERATURE.

HEBREW VISIONS: The Revelation of Moses—The Revelation of R. Joshua ben Levi—Minor Visions—The Books of Enoch—Additional Notes (Ascension of Isaiah, Baruch, Zephaniah).

CHRISTIAN VISIONS: The Apocalypse of Peter — Barlaam and Josaphat—The Passion of St. Perpetua—The Acts of Thomas—The Apocalypse of Paul—Minor Visions . 101

CHAPTER V.

EARLY CHRISTIAN LEGENDS.

St. Carpus—St. Macarius—St. Brandan . . . 157

CHAPTER VI.

MEDIÆVAL LEGENDS.

The Soldier of Gregory the Great—St. Salvius—St. Furseus—St. Barontus—Drihthelm—A Letter of St. Boniface—Wettin—A certain English Presbyter—St. Anschar—Bernold—The Emperor Charles III.—Walkelin—The Icelandic "Song of the Sun"—Alberic—The Child William—Tundal—Owain in St. Patrick's Purgatory—A Cistercian Novice—Bruno, a Chaplain of Magdeburg—A Monk of Evesham—Thurcill—St. Christina . . 171

CHAPTER VII.

CONCLUSION.

Godfried 269

FORERUNNERS OF DANTE.

INTRODUCTION.

IT is just a hundred years since Dante enjoyed unchallenged the credit of having not only composed but invented the various pictures of his *Divine Comedy*. The first serious assailant of his originality was a countryman of his own, one Francesco Cancellieri,[1] who in 1814 accused the poet of copying his details of Purgatory and Hell from a certain manuscript which his learned critic then published for the first time. This manuscript tells a story from the beginning of the twelfth century of a vision, chiefly of Purgatory, revealed to a boy named Alberic in his tenth year, and revised by him for publication later in life, after he had taken the monastic vow. Four years after the appearance of his work, ridicule was poured upon this theory of Cancellieri in no measured terms by the author, Ugo Foscolo, of an article in

---

[1] *Osservazioni sopra l'Originalità della Divina Commedia di Dante*, Rome, 1814. The MS. was discovered in 1801, and canvassed in the continental journals before its publication.

the *Edinburgh Review*.[1] Of the *Osservazioni* the reviewer there says: ". . . all that its readers can make out with certainty is, that the learned author had selected this curious subject chiefly to astonish the world by his multifarious erudition, in a book which might have been not inaptly entitled 'De rebus omnibus, et de quibusdam aliis.'" But however wrongly directed Cancellieri's attack may have been, and however ridiculous his conclusions, it would be equally absurd to suppose that there is no truth underlying his contention. There were not long wanting other works upon saner lines to show whence Dante derived, or may have derived, much of the skeleton of his plot. Ozanam and Labitte are two of the greatest names in this line of research, and copious reference will later be made to their works. It is hardly necessary to state that Dante, like every other writer before or since, drew upon the sum-total of human knowledge as it existed in the period at which he wrote. "Il trouvait cette tradition" says the former of the writers just mentioned "dans un cycle entier des légendes, de songes, d'apparitions, de voyages au monde invisible, où revenaient toutes les scènes de la damnation et de la béatitude. Sans doute il devait mettre l'ordre et la lumière dans ce chaos, mais il fallait q'avant lui le chaos existât." The object of this essay, then, is to make some attempt at constructing, from visions only, the idea of Heaven, Purgatory, and Hell which was current at the beginning of the fourteenth century; not, be it

[1] Vol. xxx. September 1818. Article "Dante."

INTRODUCTION

distinctly understood, the idea which was actually present to the mind of the Florentine. For this latter task the will and, which is even more important, the capacity are alike disclaimed. The purpose of these pages is merely to trace from their earliest beginnings the general notions of a future life, to follow their main line of development, and roughly to present the full-grown conception as it most commonly occurred at the time of its greatest and immortal exponent. References to the *Divine Comedy* will of course be made, but they must be taken as quite gratuitous, merely incidental illustrations. The present research is not conducted from Dante backwards, but from the infancy of the idea forwards to the master interpreter as a convenient stopping-place and climax.

Mention should also be made of certain further limitations of the scope of the essay. The course here taken starts with the legends of Babylonia and Egypt, comes down through those of the Greeks, the Romans, and the Jews, and finishes in the literature of the Romance languages. It has not escaped notice that there are other countries and other tongues. India and China have their own hells, and stories of men who have visited them. The *Sacred Books of the East* attest the fact. But it has been felt that these are far enough away from the mediæval conception, both in themselves and in the effect of their influence, to be safely left out of account in a study of such dimensions as the present research. Again, even after deliberately choosing a line of investigation, it is found that the side-tracks are numerous and alluring. One of these leads into the fascinating realm of antique cartography. The old map-drawers never hesitated to insert a Paradise in their charts, or an entrance to Purgatory or Hell. The Island of the Dead figures largely in these, a conception which has lasted long, and in the sphere of fancy and art has outlived the rebuffs of science; witness Böcklin's beautiful picture which bears its name. Even apart from maps, the geography of the other world raises many interesting questions. Another excursus might have been made in the direction of Parody. The Norman Fabliaux [1] yield plentiful material, and the land of Cocaigne [2] would be interesting to explore. Again, a history of our subject might be written from the point of view of pictorial art, or of sculpture, or of architecture. Scenes from a future life have been popular amongst artists and sculptors from the time of the Egyptian vignettes, and of the sculptures described by Pausanias. In none of these directions, however, has anything been attempted, with the solitary exception of a slight dip into Greek parody, whither Aristophanes beckoned too enticingly. The avowed principle which has governed our selection of material is ethical; and it is obvious that it is not in these side-issues that the eschatology of the history of visions chiefly lies.

We have spoken of the earliest beginnings of the ideas of a future life, which suggests one or

[1] See Thomas Wright, *St. Patrick's Purgatory*, p. 47 *seq*.
[2] *Ibid.*, p. 53 *seq*.

INTRODUCTION

two observations upon the genesis of such literature. The literature of visions of the dead is a necessary outcome of the universality of Religion. We may take Professor Tylor's [1] word for it that "the assertion that rude non-religious tribes have been known in actual existence, though in theory possible, and perhaps in fact true, does not at present rest on that sufficient proof which, for an exceptional state of things, we are entitled to demand." Let us borrow the same writer's "minimum definition of religion." All that he demands is a belief in spiritual beings, which he divides, in the natural and obvious manner, into two classes, the human spirit or soul, and those other spirits, of birds or trees, of stocks or stones (or of nothing material at all, indeed), which have from time immemorial peopled the demonology, theocracy, and fairyland of the human race. Now, even when religious belief meant so much and no more, the phenomena of sleep and death demanded to be explained in a manner that would fit into this animistic theory. When the spirit left the body, as it was believed to do, lying motionless in sleep or unconsciousness or death, whither did it go? When the dead warrior's wraith appeared at his son's bedside and gave him counsel or warning, whence did it come? In short, where did the spirits reside when they were not visibly and sensibly animating the bodies to which they properly, for a time at least, belonged, and where did they reside after they had finally discarded their fleshly prison, if they did not im-

[1] *Primitive Culture*, vol. i. chap. xi. p. 378.

mediately take to themselves another? That the primitive belief allowed some existence somewhere to these spirits is quite certain. It is not necessary to instance how savage peoples, and peoples not very savage too, have buried food and weapons with their dead, or entombed a man's wives with his corpse, or shown anxiety for the departed spirit's welfare in a hundred other ways. It would also be superfluous to take the witness of custom in support of the doctrine of exterior spirits, angels and demons, fairies and elves, and the like. Where, then, is this spirit-land? beneath the earth? beyond the sunset? or perhaps above the sky? Again, questions even more urgent, what is the nature of the land? and what the conditions of the life which the spirits, and especially the shades of the departed, do therein lead?

Another point which inevitably arose was the duration of the soul's life after the death of the body. Was the spirit immortal, imperishable? Did it, too, after a time die and become extinct? Or did it after a while return to this world in another form, the animating principle and essence of another body, be it human or otherwise? There were not long wanting answers to these and similar inquiries from imaginative minds who had been carried in fancy to behold the manner of life of their dead in the unseen world.

The idea of punishment and reward in a future life for deeds done in the body appeared very early. The most savage peoples have probably always had at least some rudimentary standard of right and wrong. There were certain acts which might be done with impunity, others which might not, and which were followed in this life by revenge if not by punishment. If there is retribution here, why not there, in that shadow-world, which very soon came to reflect all the various phases of this mortal life? Possibly at a later stage of development this reasoning was backed by argument suggested by a sense of fairness. The wicked might flourish as the green bay-tree, but his time was coming! One of the earliest forms of punishment after death was annihilation. The wicked soul was judged unworthy to continue its existence, and was cut off for ever. This is a primitive belief, though it was shared by a highly civilised people, the Egyptians; indeed, the general doctrine of extinction occupies a considerable place in eschatological history.

Such being, in briefest outline, the beginnings of the literature with which we have to deal, it is manifest that it is practically coextensive with the known history of mankind; for sacred writings are amongst the earliest and most carefully preserved. Of its bulk in the Middle Ages some hint will be given at the proper place. It only remains, then, to reassert the plan of this essay, which is to present such a series of visions of the future state of the dead as may give some adequate representation of the ideas of punishment and reward as they developed through the ages, and so to lead the reader up to the conception which, roughly speaking, prevailed over Europe at the time when Dante wrote his *Divine Comedy*.

CHAPTER I.

BABYLONIAN AND EGYPTIAN LITERATURE.

Gilgamesh: Ea-bani.

THE earliest legend of which we have any account is found on the tablets from Ashur-bani-pal's library at Nineveh, which date from the seventh century before Christ. This date, however, by no means represents the real antiquity of the legend, which is Babylonian, not Assyrian. According to Mr. King,[1] of the British Museum, (who has recently made this story and others very accessible in his handbook on *Babylonian Religion and Mythology*), the story goes back at least to the twentieth century, and probably a great deal further, to the Sumerian or pre-Semitic period of Babylonian myth. The legend is in the form of a poem in twelve tablets, concerning the deeds and prowess of the hero Gilgamesh, "the most prominent heroic figure in Babylonian mythology." Of this long poem only the last four tablets concern us, and even those not

[1] Mr. King's account is quoted here. Since this chapter was written, has appeared Dr. Jeremias' *The Babylonian Conception of Heaven and Hell*, ("The Ancient East" series, No. IV., translated by Miss Hutchison), which gives most instructive versions of this and the two following stories.

BABYLONIAN LITERATURE 9

very immediately. But it has been thought worth while to insert the story, both because it is the oldest extant of its kind, and for other reasons which will presently appear.

Briefly, the events which lead up to the ninth tablet are these: Ea-bani, a gigantic man with the legs of a beast, is miraculously created as a rival to Gilgamesh, under whose tyranny the city of Erech is groaning. Persuaded to leave his haunts in the woods amongst the beasts of the field, he goes to Erech, desiring first to fight Gilgamesh and then to become his friend. Both heroes, however, are warned by the gods in dreams not to fight, and accordingly they become fast friends. Thus the third tablet. In the sixth, Gilgamesh incurs the wrath of the goddess Ishtar, by scorning her proffered love. The offended deity persuades her father to create an enormous bull to destroy the hero, but in the combat which follows Ea-bani holds the bull by the tail while Gilgamesh kills it. Ishtar's anger is next turned upon Ea-bani, who threatens her with a fate somewhat similar to the bull's. At the end of the eighth tablet Ea-bani dies of a wound; and though the text is not sound, Mr. King says, "We may reasonably conjecture that his death was brought about by Ishtar, whose anger he had aroused." Gilgamesh we find "smitten with a sore sickness, which no doubt was also due to the anger of the great goddess whose love he had scorned."

In the ninth tablet, then, Gilgamesh laments his friend, and sets out to seek his ancestor, Tsit-naphishtim, (the Babylonish counterpart, or rather original, of Noah), to inquire how he himself may escape the fate of death. First he came by night to a mountain gorge, full of lions, where he prayed to the Moon-god, who showed him in a dream the pass over the mountains. Next he reaches the still greater "Mountain of the Sunset," guarded by monsters and "Scorpion-men." To one of the latter, who looks friendly, Gilgamesh describes his purpose. Warned of dangers ahead, but not discouraged, he is admitted into the mountain, and begins his twenty-four hours' journey through its thick darkness. Emerging at the other side again into the light of the sun, he sees wonderful trees laden with gems, and beyond them the sea which he has to cross. So far the ninth tablet.

An interview with Sabitu, the princess of the shore, results in his being referred to an ancient mariner, Arad-ea by name, who consents to make the passage. Gilgamesh, at his order, cuts down a tree and makes a rudder for the ship. A journey of one month and five days is then performed with miraculous speed, so that in less than three days the heroes reach the "Waters of Death." The dangerous passage of these is successfully negotiated by their combined efforts, and, approaching the further shore, Gilgamesh pours his story into the ears of his ancestor.

Tsit-naphishtim, however, regrets that he can be of no use to Gilgamesh.

> "The Anunnaki, the great gods, decree fate,
> And with them Mammetum, the maker of destiny,
> And they determine death and life,
> But the days of death are not known."

The eleventh tablet is quite detachable from its context, and, from the present point of view, irrelevant. (In answer to Gilgamesh's question how Tsit-naphishtim himself had escaped death, the latter recounts the story of the deluge, in which he had played the part of the Hebrew Noah, and tells how the god Bel had immortalised him and his wife when he took them out of the ark.) Gilgamesh is next cured of his disease by this immortal pair. The husband bids him sleep, which he does, still in the boat, for six days and six nights; during this time the wife prepares and administers to him magic food, and the cure is completed, on his awaking, by washing his sores in a healing fountain. Tsit-naphishtim had already denied, as we saw, that he can help Gilgamesh in his quest; but now, at his wife's instigation, he tells the hero where to find a magic plant which will prolong life. For some reason not stated, Gilgamesh did not at once eat the plant, and by this want of foresight, or of appetite, he lost the plant and his chance of immortality. While he was drinking at a stream, a demon in the form of a serpent snatched away the charm. Without further memorable adventure the hero regains his city of Erech.

Even the bare bones of such a story take some time and space in the telling, and so far are not very directly relevant to our subject. Gilgamesh did not properly penetrate to the realms of the dead, though he crossed the Waters of Death; he did not see on the other shore any souls of the departed, his object being accomplished when he had reached the secluded abode of his immortal ancestor. But it seems advisable to take some cognisance of his story, both for its own sake and as it explains the identity of Ea-bani, who, in the twelfth tablet, actually does return from the dead, and holds converse with Gilgamesh. This meeting was the answer to the latter's prayers to Nergal, the god of the dead, who "caused the spirit of Ea-bani to come forth from the earth like a wind." The land of the dead was a most dismal place, according to Ea-bani's account, "where was the worm which devoured, and where all was cloaked in dust." Unfortunately the text of the passage is imperfect, but Mr. King quotes the concluding passage of the poem, where we have the contrast, afterwards to become familiar in Greek literature, between the state of the buried and unburied warrior:

"On a couch he lieth
    And drinketh pure water,
The man who was slain in battle—thou
    And I have oft seen such an one.
His father and his mother (support) his head
    And his wife (kneeleth) at his side.
But the man whose corpse is cast upon the field—
    Thou and I have oft seen such an one.
His spirit resteth not in the earth
The man whose spirit has none to care for it—
    Thou and I have oft seen such an one.
The dregs of the vessel, the leavings of the feast,
    And that which is cast out upon the street are his food."

There are obviously no sufficient data for the construction of an Inferno here. It should, however, perhaps be noticed, before leaving these two visits, that Ea-bani's spirit comes *out of the earth*, and that Gilgamesh penetrated the Mountain of the Sunset, which probably also signifies a subterranean situation. If it does not, if it is preferred to suppose that Gilgamesh merely travelled to the extreme west, and did not descend into the depths of the earth, it is enough to say that it is a commonplace of primitive animism to locate the abode of the shades beyond the setting sun. It is hardly necessary to call attention to the absolute materialism of Ea-bani's report: indeed, his facts are so meagre that they barely justify comment.

Ishtar.

To Ashur-bani-pal we are likewise indebted for the preservation of the "Lay of the Descent of Ishtar." This goddess, whose acquaintance we have already made, is described as decending to the realms infernal to recover her dead lord Tammuz:

"To the land whence none return, the place of darkness,
Ishtar the daughter of Sin inclined her ear.
The daughter of Sin inclined her ear
To the house of darkness, the seat of the god Irkalla,
To the house from which none who enter come forth again,
To the road whose course returns not.
To the house wherein he who enters is excluded from the light,
To the place where dust is their bread, and mud their food
They behold not the light, they dwell in darkness,
And are clothed like birds in a garment of feathers;
And over door and bolt the dust is scattered."[1]

---

[1] See King, *op. cit.*, p. 178 *seq.*; Sayce, Hibbert Lectures, 1887, Lect. IV.; and Salmond's *Christian Doctrine of Immortality* (4th ed.), p. 65 *seq.*

Space forbids continuous quotation. The porter announces Ishtar's presence at the gates to Allatu, queen of the under world, and after a little delay he is sent back to admit her, with orders to "strip her also according to the ancient rules."

> "The First Gate he made her enter and shut (it) and he took the great crown from off her head."

To her very natural inquiry as to the reason of this proceeding, the porter's only answer is,

> "'Enter, O Lady, for thus are the laws of Allatu.'"

And so Ishtar fares at the six other gates, losing her earrings, her necklace, the ornaments of her breast, the gemmed girdle of her waist, the bracelets of her hands and her feet, and finally the cincture of her body. Next she pours forth her request to Allatu "with oaths," but the latter is "haughty before her," and orders the demon of the plague to strike her sixty times with disease.[1]

Ishtar, however, was the goddess of love, and her presence on earth could not be dispensed with. Man and beast alike neglected the function of reproduction in her absence, and accordingly the god Ea created a special messenger whom he sent to Allatu to demand Ishtar's release. The messenger asks for the Waters of Life to pour over Ishtar, and obtains them, though Allatu wreaks her vengeance, in the shape of a terrible curse, upon him, the unfortunate messenger. The queen then despatches

---

[1] Indicating thereby, as Dr. Jeremias points out, (*op. cit.*, p. 9), "that death is the destruction of all the senses, and that all that is of the body must fall to corruption."

Namtar, her own messenger, to pour the Waters of Life over Ishtar and release her once more into the upper air. At each of the seven gates of the under world the goddess receives back the part of her apparel which had there been taken from her, so that she re-emerges gorgeously attired, as when she first knocked at the portal of Hades. It should be noticed also that Namtar's instructions include this line:

"Bid the spirits of earth come forth, and seat them on a throne of gold."

These are the spirits who guard earth's golden treasure in the realms below, (as the Nibelungen, centuries later, guarded their stolen hoard), and the Waters of Life are amongst their treasures. The last three lines of the poem contain a reference to Tammuz.

It is perfectly clear that we have here the parent of the large family of legends which have from the earliest times dressed in their poetry the natural facts of the return of the seasons. But it is also clear that this, the earliest of the family, is, as we have it, a very old and a composite myth. If the story is that Ishtar, the goddess of love, seeks her dead bridegroom in Hades, then why is she herself stripped of her ornaments and gay dress as she descends, and why is she detained in Hades and smitten with sickness? Professor Sayce, in the lecture above quoted, concludes from this and from other evidence that Ishtar was once herself the goddess of the earth before she became the goddess of love, a conclusion which makes the whole story simple and obvious. Earth descends to Hades for the winter, losing all her flowers and crops, and returns gaily decked in spring. Later, then, the Tammuz legend was incorporated, probably from Egypt, by an identification of Ishtar and Isis, and, once married to the original legend, gave birth to a numerous offspring of myths and ceremonies which have lasted up to the present day. Ceremonies can still be seen which are the direct lineal descendants of the fable of the death of Osiris. References in classical literature are frequent, and in the Bible perhaps the most remarkable is that of Jer. xxii. 18:

"Ah me, my brother, and Ah me, my sister! Ah me, Adonis, and Ah me, his lady!"

Compare this with the cry of the goddess Tillili in our poem:

"O my brother, the only one, do not destroy me,"

and with the mourning for the "only son" in Amos viii. 10.

But further reference to Professor Sayce's fascinating lecture is impossible here, as all we are vitally concerned with is the matter of the "Lay." When we turn to this we find that there is not a great deal to add to Ea-bani's Hell. We have again the darkness, the gloom, and the dust.

Ishtar's case is, of course, a special one, and therefore, if we argue from it alone, we must not press our points too far, but there are one or two features of her experience that call for remark. She had to appear naked before Allatu, queen of the under world, and in this there may be some moral significance. In later visions the idea is common and important. Considerable use is made of it, for instance, in the story of Thespesius, from Plutarch, to which further reference will be made. Retribution, again, is perhaps foreshadowed in Ishtar's punishment by the plague-demon,[1] notwithstanding the fact that there were special reasons for Allatu's annoyance. Here Hell is, for the first time, called the Land of No-Return, a name which constantly recurs in later accounts. The materials, however, from the sources discussed, are still too meagre for anything like a considerable construction of the realms of the dead.

The annual sojourn of Tammuz with the dead, as distinct from Ishtar's descent, calls for no special comment. It is not a "visit" in our sense of the term. Tammuz indeed returns from the dead, but not in order to give an account of what he has seen, nor do we anywhere find such an account. For the same reason no more will be said of Osiris, nor of Adonis, nor of any other of the many names under which the hero of this myth figures in various countries and different ages.

Minor Legends.

The story of Etana's ascent to heaven on the back of his friend the Eagle[2] might contain some

[1] But the primary significance of this appears to be the corruption of death, see above, p. 14, note.
[2] King, *op. cit.*, p. 184.

information if it were complete; but, unfortunately, both the hero's neck and the tablet are broken before anything has been given which amounts to a description of the place which he visited.

There is one more story in Mr. King's book [1] which should perhaps be briefly summarised. Adapa, the son of Ea, is fishing when his boat is overturned by Shutu, the south wind. In revenge he seizes her and breaks her wings, so that she can no longer blow. Anu, the god of heaven, summons him to heaven to explain his behaviour. His father bids him dress in mourning to propitiate Tammuz and Gishyida, the gods who stood at heaven's gate, and warns him not to touch the "Meat of Death" and "Water of Death" which would be offered to him. The proffered garment he might wear, and with the oil they would give him he might anoint himself. Adapa, primed with these instructions, is admitted by the heavenly porters to Anu's presence, and on their intercession is pardoned. Anu then decides that, as he has seen the inside of heaven, Adapa must join the ranks of the gods, and accordingly orders the "Meat of Life" and the "Water of Life" to be put before him. These, however, he naturally supposes to be the fare against which his father had specially warned him, and as naturally he will have none of them. Thus he loses his chance of immortality.

This heaven is obviously nothing more than an Olympus, an abode of the blessed gods. As a

[1] P. 188.

human being, Adapa could not stay there. We further gather that the gods had "power to add to their number," but the importance of the story to our subject is extremely slight.

Setme.

By far the most complete and, so to speak, Dantesque visit to the dead in Egyptian literature is one which has been recently found on the verso of a couple of Greek official documents of the first century of our era. If any defence is needed for its insertion at this point, it is that the story is saddled upon the son of Rameses II., and therefore in a sense goes back to his date, 1300 B.C. The following account of the story and quotations from it are taken from Mr. F. Ll. Griffith's *Stories of the High Priests of Memphis*,[1] and in the main from chapter iii. of that work. The two Greek manuscripts contain a register of land, and bear the date of the seventh year of the Emperor Claudius, *i.e.* 46–47 A.D.: these have been joined together to receive the demotic narrative on the back, and it is safe to attribute this latter to the second half of the first century. The manuscript is not perfect, but fortunately most of what is gone concerned the beginning of the story and is irrelevant to our immediate subject.

It appears, then, that the wife of Setme Khamuas, son of Pharaoh Usermara (the throne

[1] Clarendon Press, 1900. Mr. Griffith indicates by his brackets uncertain renderings of corrupt words, and conjectural restorations.

name of Rameses II.), after being for some time childless, bore to her husband a very precocious son, who was called Si-Osiri. The boy was a prodigy from his earliest years; for—" It came to pass that when the child [Si-Osiri was in his first year, one] would have said 'he is two years old,' and when he was in his second [year], one would have said, 'he is three years old.' . . . The child grew big, he grew strong, he was sent to the school (?) . . . He rivalled the scribe that had been appointed to teach him." This youthful prodigy was accustomed to be taken before Pharaoh and his nobles, whom he greatly delighted.

One day while Setme and his son were attending the ἑορτή at Pharaoh's court, they saw two bodies being carried past the place for burial. One corpse was evidently that of a rich man, and was followed by the customary wailing crowds; the other was wrapped in a mat, and no one went after it to the grave. Setme's comment was this: " By [Ptah, how much better it shall be in Amenti for great men (?)] for whom [they made glory (?) with] the voice of [wailing] than for poor men whom they take to the desert-necropolis [without glory of funeral]!" His son, however, rebuked him in these rather curious words: "[There shall be done unto thee in Amenti] like [that which] shall be done to this poor man in Amenti; [there shall not be done unto thee that which shall be done to this rich man in Amenti]. Thou shalt [go (?)] into Amenti [and thou shalt see . . ." and here for thirteen lines the text is bad. It appears, however, that Setme was troubled by his son's prediction, and that the pair set out for the Necropolis. Arrived there they penetrated to the under world by the mystic entrance of the Tê. They pass through three halls of the lower regions, and the text is good again by the time they reach the fourth.

"[They entered the fourth hall] . . . [and Setme saw some men that were scattered and apart, they being also ravenous (?)]; there being also others whose food, water, and bread were hung over them, and they were hastening to take it down, but others dug pits at their feet to prevent their reaching it.

"They entered the fifth hall, and behold! Setme saw the noble spirits standing in their places, and those who had charges of violence standing at the entrance praying; [and] one man in whose right eye the bolt of the door of the fifth hall was fixed, he praying, he uttered great lamentation.

"They entered the sixth hall, and behold! Setme saw the gods of the [council (?)] of the dwellers in Amenti standing in their places, the attendants (?) of Amenti standing and making proclamation.

"They entered the seventh hall, and behold! Setme saw the figure of Osiris, the great god, seated upon his throne of fine gold, and crowned with the *atef* Crown, Anubis, the great god, being on his left, and the great god Thoth on his right; and the gods of the council of the dwellers in Amenti were standing to left and right of him. The balance was set in the midst before them, and they were weighing the evil deeds against the good deeds, the great god Thoth recording, and Anubis giving the words to his colleague. For he of whom it shall be found that his evil deeds are more numerous than his good deeds is delivered (?) to Ama of the lord of Amenti; his soul and his body are destroyed, and she (?) does not permit him to live again for ever. But as for him of whom it shall be found that his good deeds are more numerous than his evil deeds, he is taken among the gods of the council of the lord of Amenti, his soul going to heaven with the noble spirits, and he of whom it shall be found that his good deeds are equal to his evil deeds, he is taken amongst the excellent (?) spirits that serve Sokari-Osiris.

" And Setme saw (there) a great man clothed in raiment of byssus, near to the place in which Osiris was, he being of exceeding high position (?).

" Setme marvelled at those things which he saw in Amenti. And Si-Osiri walked out in front of (?) him; and he said to him, 'My father Setme, . . .'" but the precocious child is somewhat prolix, and it is unfortunately necessary to condense his explanatory comments upon what had been seen. The "great man," then, was explained to be the poor man whom they had seen being carried out for burial, and it had been commanded "before Osiris" that he should be endowed with the rich man's burial outfit, whereas the rich man was he whom the visitors had seen and heard praying and lamenting with the pivot of the gate of the fifth hall of Amenti fixed in his right eye.

These "dooms" were awarded upon the issue of

the weighing of the good deeds of the two dead men against their evil deeds, the process which Setme and his son saw being performed by Anubis and recorded by Thoth in the seventh hall of Amenti. Thus was Si-Osiri's prediction as to his father's treatment in the under world like to be justified.

His youthful guide next explains to Setme who are the inhabitants of the fourth hall. " It is just, my father Setme, these men that thou sawest scattered (?) and apart (?) they being also ravenous (?), they are the kind of men on earth who are under the curse of God, and do work night and day for their living, while moreover their women rob them and they find not bread to eat. They came to Amenti: their evil deeds were found to be more numerous than their good deeds: and they found that that which happened to them on earth happened to them in Amenti—both to them and to those other men whom thou sawest, whose food, water, and bread is hung over them, they running to take it down while others dig a pit at their feet to prevent them reaching it: they are the kind of men on earth whose life is before them, but God diggeth a pit at their feet to prevent them finding it."

No apology is needed for quoting this passage at length. The simple beauty of its style, and the terrible pathos of its hopeless fatalism, combine to produce a most striking effect. It comes like a dull moan of pain across the centuries. Was there ever so deplorable a doctrine of God, so sad a doctrine of man's future? God "diggeth a pit at their feet" in this life, and the life to come is nothing but an endless mimicry of their innocent and inevitable failure. They are denied even the comparative blessing of annihilation which is the doom of those who sinned on their own initiative. And the child-guide says " It is just."

There are several curious points in the classification of the dead in the account of Si-Osiri. To begin with, in addition to the two ordinary classes, good and bad, there is a third which is certainly uncommon apart from any mention of a purgatory. The tongue of Anubis' balance sometimes hangs straight; hence the indifferent, the Laodiceans, so to speak, who are by no means treated with the unsparing severity which they meet at the hands of St. John the Divine. Here they are but a little lower than the noble spirits who go to heaven among the gods of the council of the lord of Amenti. This threefold scheme would apparently cover all conditions of men; it has been shown, however, that the outcasts, who were from the beginning of their life predestined to endless tortures of Tantalus, form a fourth class. But the Egyptian Dives, groaning with the pivot of the gate turning in his right eye,—how is he to be classified? The treatment of Lazarus is logical and consistent: he is taken "among the noble spirits as a man of God that follows Sokari-Osiris, his place being near to the person of Osiris." That is to say, Anubis found his good deeds heavier than his evil deeds, and he became a god of the council; his fate agrees with what the travellers saw in the seventh hall of Amenti. But according to what they saw there, Dives should have been handed over for annihilation to Ama (or Am-met), the mistress of Amenti, the monster of the Judgment Scene,[1] which stands behind Thoth near the scale, and devours the unjustified. It seems impossible, then, to place Dives in a satisfactory way: he must be compared to Tityos and his brethren of the *Odyssey*, exceptionally situated as a type of penal suffering.

For the seven halls of Amenti it is perhaps worth while comparing the seven Arits or gates in chapter cxliv. of the *Book of the Dead*, and the seven gates at which Ishtar gradually lost all her ornaments in the Babylonian legend already treated. It is perhaps significant that Si-Osiri answers "never a word" to his father's question, "Is the place by which we descended different from the place whence we came up?" The mystery of the approaches to Hades appears to have been too sacred for divulgence, and in the same spirit the scribe writes of Setme concerning the whole vision, "these things weighed upon him, and to none on earth could he reveal them."

The moral tone of the legend is undoubtedly high, so much so as to make Mr. Griffith talk of Christian influence. The most conspicuous marks of advance from the *Book of the Dead* are the difference in the task of Anubis the weigher, and the absence of reference to the negative confession made to

[1] Frontispiece of Budge's *Book of the Dead*.

the assessors of Osiris in the older Egyptian system.

In the *Book of the Dead* there are two different accounts of the weighing process, which may be very briefly summarised as follows. In one [1] the body of the deceased is weighed against his heart, probably to ascertain if the former has obeyed the directions of the latter. The other,[2] the more important, Dr. Budge describes as the weighing of the heart, representing the conscience of the deceased, against a feather, the emblem of Right and Truth. Mr. Griffith, however, sees in this an idea akin to the negative confession,[3] a weighing against no weight only giving a negative justification. It is hardly necessary to point out how far ahead of this ethically is the weighing of good deeds against bad. It is the first appearance of a truly moral standard of judgment.

Again, it has been observed that in our present text the negative confession is omitted. True, the forty-two assessors of Osiris are there, but Egyptian morality has advanced beyond the formalism of the correct denial of forty-two sins, by which the deceased was ceremonially justified, and the priest, doubtless, financially aggrandised.

"Find it at thy heart," says Si-Osiri in conclusion, "my father Setme, that he who is good upon the earth they are good to him in Amenti, while he that is evil they are evil to him. These

---

[1] Frontispiece of Budge's *Book of the Dead*, p. 79.
[2] *Op. cit.*, frontispiece and p. 193. See, too, p. xciii. *seq.*
[3] *Op. cit.*, chap. cxxv.

things are established (?), [they shall not be changed] for ever. The things that thou sawest in the Tê at Memphis, they happen in the forty-two nomes in which [are the assessors (?)] of Osiris the Great God, [whose seat is in] Abydos, the place of Oracle (?), the dwellings of princes, ... Philae."

The essence of Setme's visit, then, is this. He found a Hell peopled by men who had never had a chance of escaping it, and a Heaven inhabited by the deified good. He saw, besides, that annihilation awaited the bad and glorification the not-bad, but not-good, the indifferent; the only principle of judgment being justification by works. The almost certain inference from the story is that all these states were eternal and irrevocable.

CHAPTER II.

GREEK AND ROMAN LITERATURE OF THE CLASSICAL PERIOD.

Odysseus.

THE Eleventh Book of the *Odyssey* bears unmistakable signs—only to speak of internal evidence—of being earlier than the vision just recorded. The most obvious of these is that there are no divisions in the Homeric Hades: good, bad, and indifferent alike are herded together in the bowels of the earth.[1] The heaven and hell of the demotic text are necessarily a later development. But, on the other hand, how infinitely more human is the *Odyssey*. Here, for the first time, does a living man hold converse with his dead: he weeps with his mother, and appeals to his sulky rival to forget his fancied wrong. The Homeric poem is essentially and in the first place human, and herein lies a large part of its greatness. What is to be said of the pageantry of the book? Of the gorgeous procession of heroes and heroines who drink the blood in turn, and acquaint Odysseus with their deeds, or ask him of their living friends? What

[1] ὑπὸ κεύθεσι γαίης.

GREEK AND ROMAN LITERATURE

of the arrangement and sequence of the drama that is enacted on the further shore of Okeanos? What must one think of the conception of the whole, the growth of centuries, perhaps, but already so perfect, or of the imagination which has already so vividly realised the unseen?

To weld the work as a link in the chain we are attempting to forge, a short examination of Odysseus' story will be necessary. When Circe sends off the traveller of many devices from her island, she bids him seek the spirit of Teiresias in Hades and hear from him of his home-coming. "To him," she says,[1] "Persephone hath given judgment, even in his death, that he alone should have understanding; but the other souls sweep shadow-like around!" And so, indeed, does Odysseus find them. These ψυχαί, which we translate by "souls," are in Hades mere εἴδωλα, or images, of their quondam human selves. The word ψυχή itself means the vital principle,—"something more than breath, but less than mind or spirit,"[2] and it is essential to the proper understanding of the Homeric Hades to remember that the Greek distinction was not between body and spirit, matter and mind, but, as it were, between body and shadow-body, between the living, breathing body, and the ghostly habitat of that living body's vital principle, that is, the same body debilitated and emptied to a mere effete image of its former glow-

[1] This and the following quotations are from Butcher and Lang's *Odyssey*.
[2] Salmond, *op. cit.*, p. 99.

ing, throbbing, lively self. For what was a living human being? It was a $\psi\upsilon\chi\acute{\eta}$ or vital principle, manifesting itself to human perception by means of flesh, blood, bones, and, we must add, wits. What occurred, then, at the coming of the dread enemy Death? According to Odysseus' account, a separation occurred,—a separation of the vital principle from the materials through which it was able to manifest itself. The vital principle lived on, the materials decayed or were burned. This vital principle was, then, very naturally supposed to survive in Hades in the likeness of the human body it had inspired, a silhouette of its former self, fleshless, bloodless, boneless, and witless,—in fact, just the life, or living shadow, of a human individual. Hear what his mother says to Odysseus of the fate of mortals when they die: " . . . the sinews no more bind together the flesh and the bones, but the force of burning fire abolishes these (on the funeral pyre) so soon as the life hath left the white bones, and the spirit like a dream flies forth and hovers near."[1] This is Achilles' estimate of his condition:[2] "Rather would I live upon the soil as the hireling of another, with a landless man who had no great livelihood, than bear sway among all the dead that are no more." "How durst thou," he has greeted Odysseus, "come down to the house of Hades, where dwell the senseless dead, the phantoms of men outworn?"

>   ἔνθα τε νεκροὶ
> ἀφραδέες ναίουσι βροτῶν εἴδωλα καμόντων.[3]

---

[1] l. 219.   [2] l. 489.   [3] l. 475.

Only through a draught of the blood from Odysseus' trench can these "strengthless heads of the dead" for a time regain their lost mental faculties; only thus are they enabled to recognise and converse with him. They by no means return to their former earthly condition of body, for when Odysseus would fain have embraced the spirit of his mother dead, thrice she flitted from his hands as a shadow, or even as a dream.[1] Agamemnon, too, stretched forth his hands in his longing to reach Odysseus,—" But it might not be, for he had now (even after his draught of blood) no steadfast strength nor power at all to move, such as was aforetime in his supple limbs."[2] But the εἴδωλον was certainly endowed by the blood with its old powers of mind, and with the physical function of speech, in contrast to the normal inarticulate squealing or gibbering of the dead, which is meant by that oft-quoted expression κλαγγὴ νεκύων. In this matter there is perhaps an inconsistency in the case of Ajax. His soul is represented as standing "apart, being still angry for the victory wherein I prevailed against him, in the suit by the ships concerning the arms of Achilles." Are we to infer that he drank the blood and then *went* and stood apart? The form of the passage does not naturally suggest this, but can we infer that *before drinking* he recognised Odysseus, and remembered the grudge he owed him? Certainly not, without convicting the poet of an inconsistency. In the case of Elpenor, the

---

[1] l. 204.   [2] l. 392.

preliminary is warrantably omitted; his body is still lying unburied, and therefore his spirit can find no rest in Hades, as Ea-bani likewise reported of Babylonian warriors in a similar plight, and it is not yet subject to the proper disabilities of the place. It is thus that in the *Iliad*[1] Patroclus appears to Achilles sleeping upon the beach of the sounding sea; the squire, too, is still in the intermediate state, and therefore able to seek out and hold converse with his earthly friend and lord.

Perhaps this is all we have any right to say about Odysseus' visit to the house of Hades, as embodying the views of Homeric times. What remains to be noticed is almost certainly the work of a later hand, and it is disappointing to find only in this disputed passage any mention of those great principles of which we are in search, the ideas of punishment and reward amongst the dead. There is further disappointment in the lines themselves.

"There I saw Minos, glorious son of Zeus, wielding a golden sceptre, giving sentence from his throne to the dead, while they sat and stood around the prince, asking his dooms through the wide-gated house of Hades."[2] Surely here at least is a definite conception of a judgment of souls, a weighing of the deeds done in the body, and a hint of corresponding penalty or prize? But no, we search in vain for the slightest indication of re-

[1] xxiii. 57 *seq*. This slight reference must suffice for Patroclus' story, which after all is a visit *from* and not *to* the dead, and contains nothing of present importance.

[2] l. 568.

sultant fate, and are reluctantly forced to the conclusion that the infernal court of Minos is but the ineffectual εἴδωλον of the great law-giver's earthly hall of judgment. "He appears as law-giver and arbitrator in the lower world, not because he sentences the ghosts to their punishments, but because men after death are represented as still carrying on the pursuits of their life in the upper world."[1]

Besides, it is evident that we have ceased to move amongst human beings in the proper sense of the words. Minos himself is the son of Zeus and Europa, and the instances of penal suffering are only those of mythical heroes atoning for mythical crimes. Heracles' εἴδωλον is seen, his phantom, girt with baldric of gold and armed with bow uneased, while the hero himself, αὐτός, "hath joy at the banquet among the deathless gods." The heaven suggested by this is no whit superior to the Babylonian retreat of the gods, where Adapa, the mortal, could not dwell. No, Tityos, Tantalus, Sisyphus, and Heracles alike are, on the eschatological side, devoid of human interest.

Pythagoras.

A vision of the underworld from the pen of Pythagoras would indeed have been of special interest, could it have survived to the present day. The doctrine of metempsychosis, for which his name is perhaps chiefly famous, might then have received a fuller and more explicit treatment than has been accorded to it by later writers to whom

[1] See Merry's note, *loc. cit.*

the theory was possibly less important. A *Descent into Hades* by Pythagoras did, however, at one time exist. Lobeck,[1] discussing the question whether the pictures of the gods in Homer and Hesiod were generally regarded as allegorical compositions, mentions the citation of the work by Hieronymus the Peripatetic as a proof that Pythagoras, at least, did not take that view. For Pythagoras relates how he saw both poets undergoing torment in Hades for their misrepresentations of the Olympic character! Delepierre[2] tells the story and refers to Christian Falster's *Amœnitates Philologicæ*,[3] where it is repeated with a further reference to Diogenes Laertius.[4] The latter writer repeats Hieronymus' story that Pythagoras had seen the soul of Hesiod bound with chains to a brazen pillar and gnashing its teeth, while Homer's shade was hanging from a tree enveloped by snakes; and both "as a punishment for what they had said of the gods." The same writer, however, proceeds to throw great discredit upon the worth of Pythagoras' testimony. He repeats a story that the great philosopher had an underground chamber built for himself in Italy, into which he retired for a considerable period, having previously arranged with his mother to send him from time to time budgets of general news. Afterwards he issued forth, from the shades, as it were, having made himself lean by a judicious

---

[1] *Aglaophamus*, bk. i. p. 156.   [2] *L'Enfer*, p. 13.
[3] Vol. i. p. 35 (Amsterdam, 1739).
[4] *De Vitis Philosophorum*, lib. viii. 19 *seq.*

process of underfeeding, and told the astonished natives everything that had happened on earth during his sojourn with the dead.

It is to be feared that this is somewhat of a digression, but one further scrap from Laertius may be allowed, which contains more borrowed information as to Pythagoras' descent to the dead. He quotes from a non-extant drama[1] to the effect that the philosopher had seen "all men who e'er had died," and that the Pythagoreans amongst them were held in great esteem—

> ". . . for that with them alone
> Did Pluto deign to eat, much honouring
> Their pious habits."

The answer in the play is by no means so flattering—

> "He's a civil God
> If he likes eating with such dirty fellows."

Er.

How far the story with which Plato ends the *Republic* may be taken to represent his own views upon the state of the dead, is of course a matter which must be open to question; nor can it be argued here, where the immediate concern is the matter of his narrative. It is, however, surely fair, from no reason beyond the mere prominence given to the vision, to infer that the philosopher recorded it at least in a spirit of complete sympathy.

[1] Aristophon's *Pythagoristes*.

Labitte[1] is of opinion that Plato happened upon the tradition during his travels, and "doubtless modified it according to his own beliefs." Jowett is disinclined to identify the hero of the tale with Zoroaster (as Clement of Alexandria did), though he admits that the myth has an Oriental flavour. It is only necessary to add, by way of preface, that all the astronomy of the vision, and there is much, is here omitted as irrelevant; but at the same time it is necessary to call attention to the very remarkable parallelism which exists between the structure of Er's spindle and the spheres of Dante's Paradise.

Er, the son of Armenius, a Pamphylian by birth, was slain in battle, but was found on the tenth day after the fight, his body undecayed amidst heaps of corrupted corpses, and was conveyed home for burial. There, on the twelfth day, lying on his funeral pile, he returned to life, and related his experiences in the world of the dead. When his soul left the body it came to a place where there were two openings or chasms in the earth opposite to two others in the heaven above. In the space between were judges seated, who sent the just to heaven by the right-hand opening, their sentence bound upon their breast, and similarly despatched the unjust, with their sentences tied on their backs, through the left-hand chasm in the earth. From the remaining two openings a constant stream of souls was arriving, their time of reward or punishment completed. These mingled joyfully

[1] "La Divine Comedie avant Dante," *Revue des deux Mondes*, Sept. 1842 (vol. xxxi. p. 707 *seq.*).

in the meadow where Er found himself, recognising friends and conversing with them. Especially did those who came from above make inquiries as to what were the things beneath, while those who had been experiencing the pains of hell listened to descriptions of the heavenly delights. The time of the souls' passage through heaven or hell was a thousand years, and once every hundred years they received the deserts of their earthly life, punishment or reward. Punishment and reward were thus tenfold, as a hundred years was, for this assessment, regarded as the length of a life. So far this is a simple division of men into good and bad, sheep and goats, but there is a third class of rather a curious nature—the very bad, the "incurable sinners," of whom Aridæus is the type, the Pamphylian tyrant who had murdered his aged father and his elder brother, besides committing many other "abominable crimes." When any of those unfortunates approached the chasm which gave exit to the meadow, "the mouth, instead of admitting them, gave a roar, . . .; and then wild men of fiery aspect, who were standing by and heard the sound, seized and carried them off; and Aridæus and others they bound head and foot and hand, and threw them down and flayed them with scourges, and dragged them along the road at the side, carding them on thorns like wool, and declaring to the passers-by what were their crimes, and that they were being taken away to be cast into hell."[1]

[1] Plato, *Rep.* x. p. 615 E. (Jowett's translation).

There are two or three very "modern" touches in this. There is quite a foreshadowing of that strange invention of terrific detail, whose palmiest days were the Middle Ages. In the men of fiery aspect Labitte sees "the ancestors of the devils of Alighieri." Here, too, the word "hell" (Tartarus) is for the first time used, and obviously to denote a place different from the purgatory where the unjust souls (of whom were the "passers-by" of the quotation) fulfilled their thousand years' pilgrimage, a place of endless torment reserved for the "incurables."

But a question immediately occurs,—What happened to the soul at the end of its journey? This the legend answers in a full and satisfactory manner. Every soul which re-emerged into the meadow had to enter upon a new earthly life, and upon each rested the responsibility of choosing what that life should be. The prophet who announces this responsibility to the souls ends his proclamation with the stirring and memorable sentence: "Virtue is free, and as a man honours or dishonours her he will have more or less of her; the responsibility is with the chooser. God is justified."[1] Lots were cast for the order of choosing, but this order did not very seriously damage the prospects of the last choosers: "there were many more lives than the souls present," and so the prophet exclaims, "Let not him who chooses first be careless, and let not the last despair." There were lives of all sorts and conditions of men and beasts. No definite character

[1] P. 617 E.

was attached to any life—that was left in the hands of the soul to make or to mar, but each life had its definite characteristic. Here was a life of tyranny lasting to the death of the tyrant, there the life of a woman famous for her form and beauty, and so forth. The importance and the difficulty of the choice Socrates urges in most emphatic terms. Men are to forsake all other knowledge, and to learn to discern between good and evil, so that they may, both here and always, choose the better life. The effect of various combinations of characteristics is to be the subject of a special study in this life. With what results is beauty seen in different cases to combine with poverty or with wealth? What are the various consequences of noble birth, of cleverness, of weakness? And so on. And further, "A man must take with him into the world below an adamantine faith in truth and right,"[1] in order to withstand the meretricious allurements of the many evil lives that will be offered to his choice.

Instances are given of known souls whom Er saw exercising their right of choice. Ajax would not be a man, but chose the life of a lion, remembering the injustice done him in the matter of the arms,—and reminding us, by the way, of the Homeric representation of this unforgiving soul. Atalanta fell a victim to the glories of the athletic life, and the last case we cannot forbear quoting in full, so excellent is the quiet humour of it: "There came also the soul of Odysseus having yet to make

[1] P. 619 A.

a choice, and his lot happened to be the last of them all. Now the recollection of former toils had disenchanted him of ambition, and he went about for a considerable time in search of the life of a private man who had no cares; he had some difficulty in finding this, which was lying about and had been neglected by everybody else; and when he saw it he said that he would have done the same had his lot been first instead of last, and that he was delighted to have it."[1] It is to be feared that there is more of Socrates and Plato in this glimpse than of Er, the son of Armenius.

There is little ethical significance in the function of the three Fates, who are pictured as superintending the ceremonial of the metempsychosis, so the souls may be followed directly " in a scorching heat" to the plain of Oblivion, a barren waste where they encamped by the river of Unmindfulness, " whose water no vessel can hold." There they drank, and, as they drank, forgot all things. Some, however, are described as drinking more than was necessary, and by these are intended those dense, stupid human beings who have less than their neighbours of that dim recollection of previous existence which, according to the familiar Platonic theory, constituted a large part of knowledge. After having drunk, the souls slept, and in the night (which, by the way, was the eleventh from the end of their wanderings, and thus coincided with the time elapsed since Er's death) there came a thunderstorm and an earthquake, and the souls

[1] P. 620 C.

were all driven up to their new lives like shooting-stars. Er, who had accompanied them all along merely as a spectator, not being allowed to take a lot, to choose a life, or to drink of the waters, awoke in the morning on his funeral pyre.

It is quite remarkable to observe how, in the hands of Socrates, this fragment of Pythagorean eschatology becomes filled with ethical import. Every word of the above abstract makes for morality in this present life, and it is the first time in the history of literature that any such legend has been definitely enlisted in the service of righteousness. This is most important, as so many of the later authors whose visions will be recorded here were familiar with Plato, and cannot but have been influenced by his attitude to the subject, if it was only so far as to imitate his method in using the vision as a literary form. Many visits to the dead were, in the Middle Ages, deliberately written and published with a very specific and express purpose, and not at all on the foundation of a dream or vision of any sort.

The nobility of the vision of Er and its insufficiency are alike bound up in its philosophy of metempsychosis. On this idea Socrates founds his inspired teaching, but it is just this idea which is quite irreconcilable with the modern notion of a soul's salvation. A heaven which at the end of a thousand years terminates in a new birth into this world, is no heaven at all. Hell becomes a purgatory, from which the rebirth will be a welcome release. True, there is a final and eternal hell reserved for those incurables who cannot be trusted with another life, an exception to the Pythagorean theory which it is a little hard to justify, but of a similar exception in favour of the just, of everlasting rest in heaven for the souls of the good, there is, there can be, no hint. It is not so much for its eschatology as for the moral teaching derived therefrom by the genius of a great preacher, that the legend of Er takes so high a place in the literature of the subject.

Scipio Africanus the Younger.

When Cicero employed a vision of the dead as a finish to his *De Republica*, it is plain that he did so in imitation of Plato, and if confirmation of this view is needed it is found in a comparison of his story with that of his greater predecessor. Not only is the literary form copied, but some of the details of the Latin vision are evidently borrowed from the story of Er. The astronomy of the two is roughly the same, and distinctly prophetic of the spheres of Dante's Paradise.

The *Somnium Scipionis* has fortunately survived in its entirety, and is a fine and interesting fragment. Scipio Africanus the younger, on his way to Carthage as military tribune under the Consul Manilius in 149 B.C., visited Massinissa, the famous king of Numidia, and was received by him with open arms. The day of his arrival was spent in mutual questionings on matters of administration and so forth, but for the whole evening, "in multam noctem," the old king talked of nothing but the elder Africanus, the conqueror of Zama, and adoptive grandfather of his guest. Scipio retired very late, with his ears full of the exploits and sayings of his grandfather, and, wearied with his journey and the long talk, fell into an unusually deep sleep. The vision which came to him in the night-watches he himself ascribes to this prolonged conversation and its single theme. It was his grandfather who appeared to Scipio " in the form," he says, " which was more familiar to me from his bust than from the life." Africanus bade the terrified dreamer be of good courage, and hand down to posterity what he was about to say.

He begins with matter which is personal to the young tribune, a prophetic forecast of his triumphs, his difficulties, and his very irregular *cursus honorum*. Pointing out Carthage, "in a certain place lofty, and full of stars, shining and bright," he foretells the speedy achievement of his grandson's fame. "Do you see that city which, constrained by me to obey the Roman people, is renewing its ancient wars, and cannot rest; to the storming of which you, barely a soldier, are now on your way? In two years, a consul, you will overthrow it, and will earn for yourself, by your own efforts, that aftername which you have hitherto worn as inherited from me."

It is only in the third chapter that the vision begins to reward our present search. Scipio is assured that there is a special place in heaven reserved for benefactors of their native land, that nothing on earth is so pleasing to God ("that chief

God, who governs all this universe ") as those associations of men which are called states, and that the rulers and preservers of these are sent from heaven, and return thither when their work is done ("hinc profecti, huc revertuntur"). The dreamer then asks the spirit of his ancestor if he is alive, and his own father Paulus and others, whom they of this earth think of as dead. "Most assuredly they are alive," is the response, "who have escaped from the shackles of the body, as it were from a prison; but that which you call life is death." This sentiment, for all that it was a commonplace of the schools, in its present context, which is not at any rate primarily philosophic, is impressive.

Paulus himself now appears and embraces his son, and it is perhaps worth notice that their salutations are performed without any of the difficulty which Homer and Vergil, followed by many others, put in the way of such natural expressions of affection in the other world! Dante's Hell is necessarily more corporeal than his Heaven or even than his Purgatory, and accordingly the tangibility (to the living traveller) of the shades of the *Divine Comedy* varies.[1]

Scipio's first question to his father produces an opinion on a point which is prominent alike in Vergil and Dante. He asks, if this that he sees really is life, why he is lingering on earth, and does not hasten to join his relatives. The answer

[1] *E.g. Inf.* xxxii. 97, compared with *Purg.* ii. 72, which latter is written in imitation of Vergil's "Ter frustra comprensa" (*Æn.* vi. 700-702). This again is copied from *Od.* xi. 204 *seq.*

is remarkable, and forms a very convincing estimate of the crime of self-destruction. Cicero doubtless found his line of argument in Plato:[1] the result is an admirable illustration of the height to which pure thought, untrammelled by sect or school, can attain. Unless it is God who sets the spirit free from the guardianship of the flesh, its way to heaven is barred; and men must keep the spirit in this guardianship until they receive the Divine release, lest they seem to flee from the function assigned to them by God. This implicit condemnation of self-murder affords a striking contrast, in tone at least, to the indeterminate lines of the Latin poet, and how much milder and more human it is than the fierce severity of Dante!

At this point occurs the astronomic interlude which, as has been already remarked, is strongly reminiscent of Plato, but is not at present relevant. Scipio asks what is the great and pleasant sound which fills his ears, and is informed that he is hearing the music of the spheres. By the sound of this, men's hearing, their bluntest sense, has been spoiled, and by imitation of it, on strings and in song, they have discovered for themselves a way back to heaven. (It is interesting to notice, by the way, unmistakable suggestions of the musical scale and octave.)

The young soldier is then taught in an interesting if somewhat lengthy passage to despise earthly fame and fix his gaze upon heaven. He looks at the small ball which is the earth, and his attention

[1] *Phædo*, 61 D.

is drawn to the infrequent and narrow spots on it which are inhabited. These again are arranged in two zones, the Northern, and the Antipodes (" in quo qui insistunt, adversa vobis urgent vestigia "). Of the Northern zone again, in which Scipio lives, how minute a portion lies near to him and his race. The territories of Rome are a little island surrounded by that sea which men call the Atlantic, the Great Sea, the Ocean,—a little sea for all its big names. Could Scipio ever hope that his fame would cross the Caucasus or swim the Ganges? The rest of the world, beyond these barriers, will never hear his name, and even amongst those who know it, how long will it survive? It cannot last through time, much less through eternity, on account of certain " eluviones exustionesque terrarum," which are to occur at a certain fixed time. Besides, Scipio is told, this permanence of fame is not only unachievable, but also undesirable, and to establish this point a rather curious argument is brought forward. What is the use of having one's name on the lips of posterity if it can never be spoken by the men who have already lived, who were not fewer and were certainly better men![1] Again,— a proof of the real evanescence of mortal glory, hardly more logical, and certainly not less fantastic: there are two sorts of year, the solar year and the astral. Now of this astral year there is but a twentieth part gone since the death of Romulus, (when the sun seemed to men to fail and to be extinguished). How many generations of men it

[1] "Qui nec pauciores et certe meliores, erant viri."

embraces, Africanus scarce dares to say. How futile, then, is that mortal fame which can only hope to endure for a tiny part of one year! Let Scipio fix his eyes above, where the eternal abode is, nor place his faith in human rewards. Virtue herself should draw him to true glory by her own charms.[1]

A little later is another passage [2] for which room must be found. "Ay, strive, and consider that not you are mortal, but this body: for you are not what that form of yours declares: but the mind of each man, that is the man: not the figure which can be pointed out with the finger. Know then that you are a God: if indeed that is a God which has life and feeling and memory and foresight, and which rules and governs and imparts motion to that body over which it had been placed in authority, as that chief God does to this universe: and as the eternal God himself imparts motion to a universe which is partly mortal, so does the everlasting spirit to the perishable body. For what always has motion is eternal: but that which gives

---

[1] "Suis te oportet illecebris ipsa virtus trahat ad verum decus."

[2] The passage is well worth quoting in the original: "Tu vero enitere, et sic habeto, non esse te mortalem, sed corpus hoc : nec enim tu is es, quem forma ista declarat; sed mens cujusque, is est quisque ; non ea figura, quæ digito demonstrari potest. Deum te igitur scito esse ; si quidem Deus est qui viget, qui sentit, qui meminit, qui providet, qui tam regit, et moderatur, et movet id corpus, cui præpositus est, quam hunc mundum princeps ille Deus: et ut mundum ex quadam parte mortalem ipse Deus æternus, sic fragile corpus animus sempiternus, movet. Nam quod semper movetur, æternum est : quod autem motum affert alicui, quodque ipsum agitatur aliunde: quando finem habet motus, vivendi finem habeat necesse est.

motion to something, but is itself set in motion from another source, when it comes to an end of motion, must necessarily come to an end of life." This theme is developed a little, and the labour and agitation of cares of state [1] are set forth as a speedier means of entrance for the spirit into its own proper home.[2]

The first thought that must occur when this fragment is compared with the myth which closes the Greek *Republic*, is that Cicero has, much more than Plato, confined himself to his specific subject. While the story of Er is a general vision of the state of the dead, the *Somnium Scipionis* is nothing more than a belittlement of personal ambition and a glorification of the life of the true patriot,—an eminently suitable climax to the work it was intended to crown. The literary form of a vision is here, but has been so pressed into the service of one great idea that little but the form is left. It cannot have escaped notice that the only ideas of a future state which the work presents are those which concern the spheres and their arrangement, and, besides, the one solitary indication that there is a special place of bliss reserved for those who have deserved well of their country. This latter, then, with one or two subsidiary ideas which have been noticed as they occurred, represents the whole content of the vision as far as it concerns the after-fate of the dead. It has seemed excusable, however, in spite of the meagreness of

[1] "Optimæ curæ de salute patriæ."
[2] "In hanc sedem et domum suam."

this immediate result, to give some account of the vision: it is valuable, clearly, for its lofty thought and spirituality of teaching, and further, it is an interesting and very early instance of the employ- of this particular literary form towards a very definite and specific end.

Æneas.

It seems a sort of desecration to pull to pieces a work of the magnitude of the sixth Æneid, and to press the poet for answers to questions which neither he nor his age were prepared to explain. But for the same reasons to attempt anything of the nature of an appreciation or eulogium of this section of his epic would be absurd, and its undying fame is ample excuse for plunging, without preface, *in medias res*. The spirit of the Vergilian *Inferno* has been expressed in one line of our own language in a way which is also beyond all praise: " Thou Majestic in thy sadness at the doubtful doom of human kind."

Labitte[1] has a few pertinent remarks on Dante's attitude to Vergil, but he has not much to say of the visit of Æneas to the shades. The half page devoted to the subject ends, however, with a very sound explanation of the distance which seems to separate Homer from the Latin poet—" C'est qu'entre l'Odyssée et l'Enéide, il y avait eu Platon." This is perhaps rather obviously true, as the question of Plato's influence on succeeding

[1] *Op. cit.*, pp. 706, 707.

thinkers is almost always merely one of degree. It is worth while, however, to pursue a line of thought that the remark suggests, in a narrower sphere than Labitte intended. Our subject does not extend to the general philosophy of Plato regarding a future state, but even if everything is neglected except the vision above related, the lineal relation of the two writers is clear. One of the most prominent, perhaps the most prominent idea in Vergil's scheme, and certainly its chief difficulty, is connected with his belief in the transmigration of souls, and it has been shown how important a place this theory took in the Pamphylian's narrative. Assuming that Vergil's metempsychosis is descended, however indirectly, from Plato's, it is clear that the latter bears a large responsibility, and that in this direction at least Labitte's remark can be endorsed.

Without this doctrine, the sixth Æneid would be freed from difficulty and inconsistency. For what would be left? Briefly, the departments of the underworld would be three in number,—Limbo, Tartarus, and the Elysian Fields. All three would be final and eternal, nor would there be any passage from one to another, that is to say, any purgatorial punishment. But the absence of the doctrine of transmigration would have another result, too, upon the book. It is hardly too much to say that the work would be shorn of almost all its glory. The doctrine was a literary necessity. On it hangs the whole prophetic review of Roman history and Roman greatness: only in virtue of it did Æneas behold the marshalling on the river bank of Rome's great sons that were to be.

Bearing in mind, then, how not only important but essential the theory of transmigration was to the author, on the literary side, is it absurd to suggest that herein lies the true explanation of his inconsistencies? May it not be that such difficulties represent the doubtful issue of the struggle between the man and the artist? that Vergil, whose beliefs, be it remembered also, were by no means as definite as those of John Knox, wrote his own creed as far as it carried him, and superimposed for poetical purposes the old traditional doctrine (which, as Ozanam[1] says, was one of the "primitive dogmas of Roman theology"). He *may* have believed it, but, which seems far more likely, he *may not*, and in this case would realise no necessity to make the latter part of the book in all points consistent with the earlier portions. The scene in the Elysian Fields would exist in the poet's mind on a somewhat different footing from the rest of the book. It is greater, has more romance and poetry, less of ethics and dogma, though no part of the work can be said to be strongly didactic.

And now to follow Æneas as quickly as may be in his passage through Avernus. Passing over for the meantime the preliminaries in connection with the Sibyl and the golden bough, and reserving also the incident of Misenus' death, we presently come into "Pluto's void halls and ghostly realms,"[2] where

[1] *Op. omn.*, vol. v. p. 508, n.
[2] The quotations are from Conington's translation.

"before the threshold, in the very mouth of Hell, Agony and the fiends of Remorse have made their lair: there dwell wan diseases, and woful Age, and Terror, and Hunger that prompts to Sin, and loathly Want — shapes of hideous view — and Death, and Suffering; then comes Sleep, Death's blood-brother, and the soul's guilty joys,[1] and deadly War couched in the gate, and the Furies' iron chambers, and frantic Strife, with bloody fillets wreathed in her snaky hair."[2] This magnificent passage needs no comment, but a word of admiration may be allowed for the genius which places this terrific group of the sources and concomitants of death at the very entrance and threshold of the underworld.[3]

With Charon and Styx, and with the rivers of Avernus in general, we are not immediately concerned: Conington's opinion[4] seems very reasonable, "that Vergil found the notion of a single river of death most convenient for poetical purposes, but that he wished as usual to introduce the various points of the legends he followed"; for this reason he varied the name and implied a plurality of rivers. This view supports that of Heyne.[5] The position of Phlegethon, however, is clearly defined, a separate river surrounding Tartarus.

[1] Conington's Vergil, vi. 278, n. "Evil pleasures ... the end of which is death." [2] l. 273.

[3] Heyne, *sub loc.* "Ingeniose in faucibus et aditu locorum inferorum constituta ea, quæ vel morti sunt vicina vel in morte sunt."

[4] l. 295 n.

[5] *Loc. cit.* "Non subtiliter et ad historici diligentiam nomina .... posuit .... sed poetæ more ea variavit."

As to Palinurus, it is only necessary to refer him to his Homeric prototype Elpenor, and to state that the death of Misenus is apparently a redundancy.[1] Palinurus' state qualified him to play Misenus' part in delaying Æneas' entrance to Avernus. The Homeric theory as to the condition of the unburied dead remains practically unaltered, except that Vergil has set a terminus of a hundred years to their restless wandering, after which "they see again the flood of their longing."[2]

When the "sea-green boat" has discharged its unwonted living freight, and the priestess, his companion, has thrown a sop to Cerberus, Æneas quickly turns his back upon the "river without return." The "Hound of Hell" is pictured[3] as assigning the souls of the dead to their proper locality by the number of coils which he gives to his tail. It seems possible that Milton had this in his mind when he wrote, of the devil, "swinges the scaly horror of his folded tail." Æneas finds himself at once in a limbo, whose five departments are peopled in a way which presents to the modern mind five separate problems in eschatology.

First, there smites the ear of the hero the wailing of infant spirits, "babes that, portionless of the sweets of life, were snatched from the breast by the black death-day's tyranny, and whelmed in untimely might." They were not "sobbing and crying" on account of any pain they suffered, but only for the loss of the sweets of life, which loss

[1] See Conington, *Æn.* vi., Intr. and l. 161 n.
[2] l. 330.   [3] See Labitte, *loc. cit.*

they were understood in some dim way to realise. What Er the Pamphylian heard on the subject of these infants he reported as unworthy of record,[1] from which it may be supposed to have been of a somewhat similar nature. Even in Dante[2] we find the same cruel doctrine as to the future of the unbaptized, who are held in painless sorrow in the Limbo of the first circle of Hell:

> "And here, so far as hearing truth might win,
>   No other plaint rose up than that of sighs,
> That made the air all tremulous within.
>   This from the sorrow without pain did rise,
> Endured by those vast multitudes and great,
>   Which infants, men, and women did comprise."

It needed the larger humanity of the Christian faith at its best and purest[3] to assign these poor innocents to their proper abode, though the Jewish belief on the subject appears to have been eminently satisfactory.[4]

"Next to them are those who were done to death by false accusation. Yet let none think that the lot of award or the Judge's sentence are wanting here. There sits Minos, the president, urn in hand: he summons an assembly of the speechless, and takes cognisance of earthly lives and earthly sins."[5]

---

[1] Plato, *Rep.* x. p. 615 C.

[2] *Inf.* iv. 26 *seq.* (Plumptre's translation).

[3] Cf. Lecky's *Rationalism*, vol. i. p. 395. "Some of the Greek Fathers, indeed, imagined that there was a special place assigned to infants where there was neither suffering nor enjoyment, while the Latins inferred from the hereditary guilt that they must descend into a place of torment; but both agreed that they could not be saved."

[4] See below, p. 114.   [5] l. 430.

GREEK AND ROMAN LITERATURE

A modern sense of fairness demands that these unfortunates should be compensated — *ceteris paribus*—for their unjust doom. But though Minos must be understood as rehearing their cases, no mention is made of any consequent amelioration of their lot, and there the matter must rest. The second sentence of the above quotation points, however, to a more real and active function for Minos than he enjoyed in the Homeric scheme, in spite of his unsatisfactory failure to deal with the case of the wrongly condemned.

In the third department of Limbo, Vergil seems to err on the side of leniency, and this was perhaps to be expected, in consideration of the views held in his time (for instance, by the Stoics). Cicero's view from the lips of Africanus, to which attention has above been drawn, must be regarded as something rather exceptionally grand, and different from, though by no means entirely in advance of, his age. Here are found "the sons of sorrow, who, though guiltless, procured their own death by violence, and, for mere hatred of the sunshine, flung their lives away."[1] They, too, like the infants, desiderate the sweets of the life to which they have, of their own misguided will, put an end. "Oh, how gladly," the poet adds, "would they now, in the air above, bear to the end the load of poverty and the full extremity of toil." Dante has a very different fate in store for these in his forest of suicides; hear how one of them describes their fate:[2]

[1] l. 434. [2] *Inf.* xiii. 95.

"'When the fierce spirit quitteth,' he began,
  'The body which in wrath it left behind,
Then Minos sends it to the seventh pit's span;[1]
  Into the wood it falls, no place assigned,
But there, where Fortune speeds its arrow's chance,
  Like grain of spelt, it buds from out its rind,
And its young shoots to forest tree advance:
  The Harpies then its tender leaves devour,
Wound, and an outlet make for utterance.
  We, like the rest, shall come in judgment's hour,
To seek, but not resume, our earthly dress,
  O'er what he casts away man loses power.
These we shall drag, and through this wilderness
  So drear each tree its several corpse shall bear
Hung on the thorn of soul in sharp distress.'"

This passage runs to the opposite extreme of severity, and few will be found to sympathise with Dante in his harsh treatment of the unhappy Chancellor of Frederick II. of Italy. But though we plead extenuating circumstances, and in certain cases come very near to condoning the act, yet there is obviously no getting over the fact that suicide is a crime, and is not appropriately treated in the practically emotionless Limbo of Vergil. Probably nowhere shall we see a better proof of the impossibility of classifying sinners under general headings. On the one hand, we are repelled by the crowning cruelty of the suffering which Dante, in obedience to the law of his classification, assigns to the spirit of Pier della Vigne, and in comparison with which the Vergilian Limbo would be heaven itself; but again, there

[1] To the second round of the seventh circle, which is the circle of Violence or Bestiality.

are many of the same class, many suicides, whose crime was a cowardly escape from a life whose hardships and duties, though these were nothing out of the common, they had not the pluck to face, and in view of such the Æneid seems inadequate.

The Mourning Fields form the fourth department of Limbo. "Here dwell those whom cruel Love's consuming tooth has eaten to the heart, in the privacy of hidden walks and an enshrouding myrtle wood: their tender sorrows quit them not even in death."[1] Together with the interview with Dido, this makes a beautifully poetic passage, but clearly Romance has altogether ousted Ethics. To refer to Dante's treatment of the same subject[2] is to compare the pagan poet with the Christian teacher. Dante faints with pity at the romantic story of Paolo and Francesca, but he is inexorable, and it is in the second circle of Hell, driven in darkness like starlings by the howling winds, and crying like cranes, that he meets them. It is impossible to credit Vergil with any ethical attitude at all; for the time at least he is lost in ancient romance, and his readers must look elsewhere for moral instruction.

The difficulty of the "separate place tenanted by the great heroes of war" is of a different nature, and consists in a clear fault of construction. Vergil has made his classes overlap one another. The present is not a moral division at all, and therefore must contradict the judgments of Minos. There were good warriors and bad warriors, warriors

[1] l. 442. [2] *Inf.*, canto v.

whose career pointed plainly to Tartarus, and others who were fit inhabitants for the Elysian Fields. But it is useless to linger on so obvious an inconsistency.

Conington, in his Introduction to this book of the Æneid, mentions the view that the general idea of this fivefold Limbo is that of a receptacle for the souls of those who have been prematurely cut off from life, and are therefore not liable to the ordinary system of judgment, penalty, and reward. This is far from satisfactory, partly because it makes Minos so ineffectual, as has been already shown, and partly because it is difficult to see that in all cases the end has really been premature. But the point is hardly worth arguing here, and this view is probably the best obtainable.

It is when Tartarus is reached, and the Elysian Fields, the Hell and Heaven of Æneas' vision, that we can calculate the sum of Vergil's teaching, and we find that, on the whole, the moral significance of the poem is rather meagre. Nor could it be otherwise. It was not the primary purpose of the work to teach morals, but rather to inculcate the greatness and majesty of Rome. The sixth Æneid, when it appeared, might have been styled a new representation in Latin verse of sundry legends dealing with the state of the dead, together with a " Gesta Romani populi "[1] introduced under the form of a prophecy. Even in Tartarus, which an examination will show to be by far the most moral part of the work, the ethical teaching is disappoint-

[1] As Servius calls it, cited by Ozanam.

ing. True, " Phlegyas, from the depth of his agony, keeps warning all, and proclaiming with a voice of terror through the shades, 'Learn hereby to be righteous, and not to scorn the gods'";[1] and it must be admitted that some of the descriptions of the criminals have a familiar and human sound. The vices of hatred, fraud, and avarice have survived up to modern times. But there is still hanging over the Vergilian Tartarus a certain amount of the ghostly unreality which was deplored above in the Homeric scheme, and Vergil's types of the damned are drawn from the same class, the heroic. Everything is on too large and too remote a scale; the everyday, human element is deficient. There is little here of terror or of hope for the individual conscience, little, at least, compared to what a didactic treatment of the same material might have produced. " All dared some monstrous crime, and enjoyed their daring."[2] This quotation, too, simply stultifies the function of Minos and Rhadamanthus: their judgments were foregone conclusions, and except that the Tartarean judge assessed the penalties of the damned, their posts were sinecures. But there is a crumb of cold comfort for the moralist in the Sibyl's final word on the subject of Tartarus. The damned cannot all have been legendary heroes such as those who are mentioned by name: "'No; had I even a hundred tongues, and a hundred mouths, and lungs of iron, not then could I embrace all the types of crime, or rehearse the whole muster-roll of vengeance.'"[3]

[1] l. 618.   [2] l. 624.   [3] l. 625.

Of the Elysian Fields much the same criticism holds good. It is not meant to imply, be it understood, that there is no moral teaching, that the doctrines of punishment and reward have not made great strides since Homeric times, but only that the ideas are made distant and unreal by their romantic treatment. In poetic value and permanent interest they gained greatly for what they lost in nearness to the human life of the time.

One significant passage may be quoted as the earliest strongly marked instance of its sort. In the apocryphal visions, and later, it will be seen that it is possible, after a fashion, to reconstruct the society of any period and place from the particular virtues and vices attached to the inhabitants of the contemporary Hades. In the passage about to be quoted, it is for the first time possible to do something specific on these lines. "Here is a noble company who braved wounds in fight for fatherland; all the priests who kept their purity while life was; all the poets whose hearts were clean, and their songs worthy Phœbus' ear; all who by cunning inventions gave a grace to life, and whose worthy deeds made their fellows think of them with love." It might be a mistake to press the inference too far, but there is at least something to be gathered from this quotation as to the character of the priestly order in Vergil's time, and as to the amelioration of the conditions of life, in fact the advance of civilisation. In touches of this sort the poet does not distinguish rigidly between his own environment and that of his hero, even when the two are not contemporary.

Reversing the actual order of the text, the incidents connected with Æneas' admission to the shades have been reserved until more relevant and important matters have been discussed. The side-question of the golden bough can be explored to the full in the intensely interesting work of Professor Frazer which bears its name. The only other point on which remark seems desirable is contained in Æneas' prayer to the Sibyl, his request for admission. "'If Orpheus,'" he urges, "'had the power to fetch back the shade of his wife, by the help of his Thracian lyre and its sounding strings,—if Pollux redeemed his brother by dying in turn with him, and went and returned on the path these many times,—why talk of Theseus, why of great Alcides? My line, like theirs, is from Jove most high.'"[1] That is to say, Æneas pleads his divine descent and the precedent established by former heroes of the same high birth as reasons why the gates of Hades should not be shut against him. This fact is mentioned as an opportunity for observing that, from the present point of view, these predecessors of Æneas do not repay minute study. The stories of Theseus and Pirithous, of Castor and Pollux, of Orpheus and Eurydice, and of a number of others who could be mentioned, are purposely excluded from the present list of descents to the shades, and for this reason: they are all, without exception, on

[1] l. 119.

classical lines, and after reading the eleventh Odyssey and the sixth Æneid there is nothing further to be learnt from them concerning the state of the dead. As Vergil copied Homer, it was only to be expected that others would imitate them both. The popularity of this form of literature in classical times may be inferred from Labitte's sentence, "À Àthenes comme à Rome chaque poète versifiait sa descente chez Pluton."[1] Of these descents A. F. Ozanam[2] gives an admirable account, which, short though it is, is very inclusive.

By way of example of what we may call the "classical" descent, take Vergil's own *Culex*,[3] if indeed it be his. In this quaint little poem, which has, by the way, an attractive beauty of its own, a shepherd lies down in the grass to enjoy an hour's repose. While he is sleeping a huge hydra sees him, and is on the point of slaying him, when a gnat saves his life by stinging him into consciousness. The shepherd's first wakeful act is to crush the gnat in his annoyance, after which he proceeds to demolish the serpent. The same night the shepherd is sleeping,

"When lo! his sight the gnat's pale form assails,
And mournful thus his cruel death bewails."[4]

---

[1] *Op. cit.*, p. 710.

[2] *Op. omn.*, vol. v. pp. 496–533 (*i.e.* chap. vi. of *Des Sources Poétiques de la Divine Comédie*). Previous to this work Ozanam had written a Latin treatise bearing the title (to quote from memory), *De frequenti apud antiquos poetas heroum descensu ad inferos*.

[3] An apology is needed for introducing this work, as it deals rather with a *return from* the dead than a visit to the lower regions.

[4] The quotation is from a particularly spirited translation of the *Culex* by Lucius M. Sargent, (Boston, 1807, 8vo).

GREEK AND ROMAN LITERATURE

The tiny spectre then proceeds to give the shepherd the regular traditional and classical account of Hades. Here are Lethe and Styx, Charon, Othos and Ephialtes, Tityos, Tantalus, "Pluto's gloomy bride," and a host of others, the stock paraphernalia of a well-established and full-bodied legend.

Thespesius.

It is no anachronism to include the works of Plutarch in the present section of our literature. There will, indeed, be occasion to refer to works of an actually earlier date, but those works are late Jewish and Christian, whereas the passages of Plutarch with which we are concerned, however high their moral purpose, are entirely classical in spirit, and thoroughly pagan. The great moralist relates two stories of visits to the dead, each in its own way strongly reminiscent of the close of the *Republic* of Plato. The latter part of *The Delays of Divine Justice* is Plutarch's vindication of the principle of vicarious punishment, which was, and indeed still is, so visible in its operation in human life. His catalogue of infernal torments is very striking: in no previous work have we met anything half so realistic or so prophetic of Dante's Hell. Labitte[1] is surely mistaken in finding traces of Christian doctrine in the work. "Nous touchions aux mystères de l'Evangile," he says, but as the scholar[2]

[1] *Op. cit.*, p. 709.
[2] Dr. Philemon Holland (London, 1603). I have modernised his spelling.

whose translation is quoted below points out, the doctrine of original sin, of the common curse of all the sons of Adam, was clearly unknown to Plutarch. It is chiefly the beneficial influence, the practical utility of vicarious punishment which he upholds; and besides, the doctrine of hereditary responsibility, of the visitation of the iniquity of the fathers upon the children, is an Old Testament dogma, and for that matter a commonplace of Greek thought, but certainly does not belong peculiarly to the New Testament.

Following a precedent now familiar to us, Plutarch closes his tract with a vision of the pains and penalties of the future life. This vision must necessarily be one-sided; it belongs to the same class as the *Somnium Scipionis*, and many others to which reference will be made; it is designed to fulfil a definite purpose; in this case to establish by circumstantial evidence a specific doctrine. The Ciceronian vision was all heaven, (what there was of it), and that with a special object; the present writer, interested primarily in vicarious punishment, may be excused for omitting to mention a heaven at all.

At Soli, in Cilicia, there lived in Plutarch's own time a certain Aridæus, a notorious debauchee, who had squandered his patrimony, and supported himself by all manner of shameful malpractices. Consulting the oracle of Amphilochus as to whether the rest of his life would be better than what was already behind him, he was told that "it would be better with him after he was dead." The oracle

was fulfilled in the following curious manner:—
Aridæus fell off a height and was killed; but three
days later, after he had been carried out for burial,
he returned to life, a changed man, conspicuous
afterwards for his honesty and devoutness as he
had previously been for his profligacy. Asked to
explain the alteration in his life and character,
Thespesius (for he brought this new name with
him from the other world) thus unfolds his tale.
When his soul first left the body, he felt like a
pilot flung from his ship, and falling to the bottom
of the sea. Gradually recovering, however, he
looked round him, "for his soul seemed as if it had
been one eye fully open," and saw a countless host
of planets and stars, of wonderful brightness and
colour, on the rays of which his soul was carried
about, "as in a chariot," whithersoever it would.
Thespesius now observed a constant ascending
stream of small bubbles of fire, each of which burst
and gave forth a soul, in human shape, but "very
light and nimble." These souls of the departed
either rise "plumb upright" to the upper regions
of the air, where they enjoy a kind of sedate calm,
or they remain huddled and clinging together,
mostly at a lower level, whirling round "like unto
bobbins of spindles." This is a sort of separation
of good and bad, but it is not complete, as we read
that the tranquillity of the souls above was much
interrupted by groups of their whirling, disorderly
fellows.

Thespesius relates that he was presently saluted
by a relative of his own who had died when he was

a child, and whom he therefore barely recognised. His kinsman knew him for a living man by the fact that he cast a shadow,[1] and because he opened his eyes and winked them, which the souls of the dead could not do. He tells the traveller that henceforth he is to be called Thespesius, not Aridæus; that he is not dead, but that "by the Providence of God and Permission of Destiny" he is come thither with the intellectual part of his soul (an unsubstantial substance surely to cast a shadow!), while the rest of his soul is left behind as an anchor to his body. Before his relative greets him, Thespesius has already in vain accosted the souls of several of his deceased friends; but the inference from this and later passages is that mutual recognition is in most cases possible (here it is necessary, in order to provide Thespesius with a guide). Like some other great writers, Plutarch is not entirely consistent.

Thespesius then proceeds to an account of the scheme of punishment whose operation he witnessed. The appearance of the souls is first described: sin leaves its mark upon their natural transparency in the shape of scars and blots, varying in number and obscurity. Some were "all-to bespecked with black spots, like to serpents' skins," while others were of a perfectly clear purity. Besides this there is a classification of wicked souls according to colour; black is the "tincture of Avarice," fiery red betokened a life of Cruelty and Malice, blue was the sign of Intemperance, which

[1] Dante, *Purg.* iii. 21 and 90.

"will be hardly scoured off, for that it is a vile vice," while those souls which had been mastered by Envy are stained with a "violet colour and sweetish withal, . . . a venomous and poisoned colour, resembling the ink that cometh from the cuttle fish."

Over all the punishments of these souls the goddess Adrastia presides, daughter of Jupiter and Necessity, and no sinner, great or small, either by force or by cunning, can escape her. She has three subordinates under her, each in charge of a separate penal function. First of the three is Poene (*Ποινή*), or Penalty, to whom is entrusted the "petty purgation" of those who have already suffered for their offences in this life, and who are really not very hopeless sinners. Next, "such as require more ado to have their vices and sins cured" are handed over to Dike (*Δίκη*), or Retribution; but those who are so laden with sin as to be quite incurable this goddess thrusts from her, and they are hunted and pursued by the third, named Erinnys. She, when she catches them, hurls them into a "bottomless pit of darkness inenarrable and invisible."

This last class clearly corresponds to the "incurable sinners" of Plato's myth. The "bottomless pit" is the Tartarus of the earlier story, and the souls which are cast into it are eternally damned. But the case of souls less soiled is more hopeful. Under the ministrations of Penalty or of Retribution, their blotches and specific colourings gradually disappear, until at length they stand "in their native hue, all fresh, clear, neat, and lightsome." So far, then, we have a sound conception of Hell and Purgatory, and, as already observed, we have no reason to expect a Heaven.

His guide next conducts Thespesius to the place of Lethe, which was a "huge wide chink, tending downward still." It "resembled for all the world, within, the caves of Bacchus," and the souls which lingered there fed on the fragrant odour of the place. This latter point is interesting, being the earliest mention in our literature of a form of ghostly sustenance which becomes very common in later visions. Thespesius is informed that "Bacchus by that way mounted up into the society of the gods, and afterwards conducted Semele," but he is not allowed to enter the cave, nor to stay any time at its entrance. The place tended to sensuality: the pleasure of it dissolved, as it were by moisture, the reasoning and intelligent part of the mind.

Next follows matter even less important, the "standing boll" into which several rivers flow, the three angels sitting "in triangular form" and mixing the variously coloured waters of the rivers. So far, it appeared, came Orpheus in his search for his wife. Nor are we concerned with Thespesius' excursus concerning the oracle at Delphi, though it should perhaps be mentioned that he heard the loud and shrill voice of a woman prophesying, amongst other things, the exact time of his own death.

"After this they passed on forward to see the

pains and torments of those who were punished." Thespesius, "who doubted nothing less," recognised many of his former intimates, amongst whom his own father rose out of a deep pit, covered with cuts and gashes, and, stretching out his hands to his son, confessed to the murder of certain guests for their gold. The crime had not been detected on earth, and accordingly its punishment was all the more severe in Hades. Thespesius retreated in fright and astonishment without daring to "make suit nor intercede" for his parent, and by so doing lost sight of his guide, whom he saw no more.

And now Thespesius remarks on what is perhaps the finest moral distinction we have yet seen. The shadows of "notorious malefactors, in the view of every man," and of those who had in this life suffered for their sins, are less severely chastised than such as were "disguised and cloaked with an outward appearance and reputation of virtue abroad, and yet had lived covertly and secretly at home in wickedness." The exposure of these specious sinners is forcibly described : "Certain that were about them forced some of them to turn the inside outward, and with much pain and grief to lay themselves open, to bend and bow, and discover their hypocritical hearts within, even against their own nature, like unto the scolopenders of the sea, when they have swallowed down an hook, are wont to turn themselves outward."

Thespesius saw, too, groups of souls, interlaced like serpents, gnawing and devouring one another. These were they who could not forget their old grudges and rancours, and they remind us very strongly of the terrible picture of the Lake of Ice in Dante's tenth circle of Hell:[1]

> " . . . in one pit I saw two frozen thrust,
> So that one head as hood to th' other grew;
> And as a famished man devours a crust,
> So there the topmost one his teeth set fast,
> Where skull with neck the juncture doth adjust."

Next the traveller arrives at the scene of the punishment of the avaricious. Here were three parallel lakes, the first of molten gold, the second of frozen lead, and the third of rough iron. These were in charge of certain demons, who, "like unto metal-founders or smiths, with certain instruments either plunged in, or else drew out, souls." There is considerable detail of imagination in the description of this torment. The victims of avarice are first plunged into the gold, and when they are "once set on a light fire, and made transparent by the flames," are dragged out and thrown into the second lake, where they are "congealed and hardened in manner of hail." The lake of iron made the souls "exceeding black and horrible," it cracked and broke them "by reason of their dryness and hardness." And then the whole process was repeated, the souls "suffering by the means of these changes and mutations, intolerable pains." If the horrors of hell far surpassed these torments of Purgatory, we do not wonder that the "bottomless pit" was "inenarrable and invisible"!

There follows what must, in view of the subject

[1] *Inf.*, xxxii. 125 *seq.*

of the latter part of Plutarch's treatise, be regarded as the central point or climax of the story. The souls which seemed to Thespesius to be the most miserably tormented were those who imagined that their punishments were done and their crimes expiated, but were seized again, and put to fresh torture. "Those were they for whose sins their children and others of their posterity suffered punishment: for whensoever one of the souls of these children or nephews [1] in lineal descent either met with them, or were brought unto them, the same fell into a fit of anger, crying out upon them, showing the marks of the torments and pains that it sustained, reproaching and hitting them in the teeth therefor; but the other making haste to fly and hide themselves, yet were not able so to do; for incontinently the tormentors followed after and pursued them, who brought them back again to their punishment, crying out, and lamenting for nothing so much as that they did foresee the torment they were to suffer, as having experience thereof already." Further, Thespesius saw these souls of "children or nephews" hanging together in clusters "like bees or bats, murmuring and grumbling for anger when they remembered and called to mind what sorrows and calamities they sustained for their sake." This picture Plutarch deliberately draws with the express purpose of softening or terrorising living parents, to coerce or persuade them to righteousness. The best com-

[1] *i.e.*, of course, descendants. The Greek words of the context are παῖδες and ἔκγονοι.

ment on it is to quote in his own words the argument in proof of which the story of Thespesius is adduced. " And considering that there is no punishment more ignominious, or that cometh nearer to the quick, and toucheth the heart more, than for men to see their offspring, or those that depend upon them, afflicted for their sake, and punished for their faults ; and that the soul of a wicked person, enemy to God and to all good laws, seeth after his death, not his images and statues, or any ensigns of honour overthrown, but his own children, his friends and kinsfolk ruinate, undone and persecuted with great miseries and tribulations, suffering grievous punishment for it; there is no man, I think, but would choose rather to forego all the honours of Jupiter, if he might have them, than to become again either unjust or intemperate and lascivious."

And now, at the end of the story, we are suddenly and for the first time, as in the sixth Æneid, confronted with the theory of metempsychosis. Here, as with Vergil, though not at all to the same extent, the idea gives trouble, and the difficulty must be explained on the same lines : the principle of transmigration is not of universal application in Hades. It would be contradictory to the spirit of the story to suppose that any soul could return from the bottomless pit to enter upon a new human life; the lesson of this, to the believer, was that it was possible so to abuse one opportunity of achieving character that no second chance would be given. Further, Thespesius only talks of " the souls of *such as* entered into a second life and new nativity," from which it is clear that not all the dead, perhaps not even all the inhabitants of purgatory, were fated to put on again a garment of flesh. Altogether, the passage is slight, and does not teach much. It has also two serious faults of construction.

In the first place, the souls were prepared for their new life by a process which must have been, to say the least of it, extremely painful. There were " certain workmen appointed therefor, who, with tools for the purpose and many a stroke, forged and framed some of their parts new, bent and wrested others, took away and abolished a third sort; and all that they might sort and be suitable to other conditions and lives." Now this is a form of torture, and it is either unfair to inflict it upon souls which have already finished their purgation, or unfair to inflict it upon those which have not: in the one case no further torment is just, and in the other a too speedy release is offered from the pains of purgatory. Secondly, and this is practically a part of the same difficulty, we find the soul of Nero already being forged and hammered into that of a snake. Surely most impartial critics would agree in handing over this soul to Erinnys and the bottomless pit; but even taking the more lenient view, is not a century rather a brief space of purgation for so much infamy? The passage is hardly worth serious comment, but the quaintness of it perhaps justifies a short quotation. " He espied the soul of Nero

... pierced through every part with spikes and nails red hot with fire; and when the artisans aforesaid took it in hand to transform it into the shape of a viper, of which kind (as Pindarus saith) the young ones gnaw through the bowels of the dam to come into the world, and to devour it, he said that all on a sudden there shone forth a great light, out of which there was heard a voice giving commandment that they should metamorphose and transfigure it into the form of another kind of beast, more tame and gentle, forging a water creature out of it, chanting about standing lakes and marshes, for that he had been in some sort punished already for the sins which he had committed, and besides some good turn is due unto him from the gods, in that of all his subjects, he had exempted from tax, tallage and tribute, the best nation and most beloved of the gods, to wit, the Greeks."

Hitherto Thespesius has been merely a spectator of the torments he has described; but now, to impress the facts the more lastingly upon his memory, a certain stately woman " put forth unto him a little wand or rod all fiery." Thespesius was rescued, however, from this harpy, and found himself " blown by a strong and violent wind with a trunk or pipe, so that, in the turning of a hand, he was within his own body again, and so began to look up with his eyes in manner out of his grave and sepulchre."

Timarchus.

The second vision related by Plutarch[1] describes the experiences of a "young gentleman," to quote from the same translator, who consulted the oracle of Trophonius as to the nature and power of the familiar spirit, or Demon, of Socrates. It belongs, therefore, to the class of visions with a purpose, and as that purpose is hardly in line with our main subject, the story need not long delay us. After the customary purifications, and with the usual rites, which are described by Pausanias,[2] the youth, whose name was Timarchus, of Chæronea, descended into the cave, and, to the great alarm of his friends, remained there for two nights and a day.

After Timarchus had lain for some time on the ground, uncertain whether he was awake or dreaming, a great noise seemed to light upon his head and split the seams and sutures of his skull, thus allowing his soul to escape. It is only charitable to suggest that to this severe blow may be due the extreme obscurity of much of Timarchus' relation! The beginning is a vision of varicoloured isles floating in a varicoloured sea, and making the sky resound with their music as they float. This is of course simply a variant of the spheres and their music, which we have already heard. These things Timarchus beheld with delight; "but when he came to look downward," he saw a huge and vastly deep hole, or gulf, "in manner of an hollow globe

[1] *De Genio Socratis*, xxi., xxii. [2] ix. 39, 5-14.

cut through the midst." It was horrible to see, and dark and turbulent, sometimes boiling outwards, and from it came countless roarings of beasts, wailings of children, and lamentations of men and women, besides many noises . . . and outcries of all sorts, and those not clear, but dull and dead, as being sent up from a great depth underneath. In this abyss Timarchus saw stars "leaping up and down . . . some drowned and swallowed up in it, others appearing again from below." These, of course, are the demons, and a detailed account of their conditions and movements, and of the interpretations of these, would not be worth the space it would occupy. The whole scheme, if scheme it can be called, is confused and obscure, and the result of it to our subject is practically valueless.

Parodies: The "Frogs."

Reference has already been made to the popularity of the descent to the dead as a theme amongst classical writers. If further evidence be desired, it is found in the fact that the subject has not escaped the pen of the comic writers of the period. Two very famous parodies survive—the "Frogs" of Aristophanes, followed at a much later date by the "Menippus" of Lucian. While the Attic comedy is of course a much greater work, for this very reason it less closely resembles and follows the form of the serious literature of the subject. With Aristophanes the parody is a literary dress in which he clothes his satire on the other subjects which he has in mind. First of these latter is the languor and decline upon which the Tragic Muse has fallen in his day, and this is the real subject of the comedy. The god Bacchus, with a slight Herculean disguise thrown over his usual effeminate attire, accompanied by a clever and unscrupulous rascal of a slave, visits the infernal regions in order to bring back from the dead the soul of Euripides. On this slender foundation the stupendous fertility of the world's greatest comic writer has constructed the "Frogs."

Clearly the descriptions of the Plutonic kingdom are only incidental. Further, they do not diverge from what have been called the "classical lines," and, in consideration of our immediate subject, it will be more profitable, and even more amusing, to turn to the ridiculous story of Lucian.

The "Menippus."

There is a vast amount of pertinent truth underlying the very humorous dialogue between Menippus and his friend Philonides. The work is an obvious burlesque of the eleventh Odyssey and of the cave of Trophonius.[1] Menippus appears disguised in a lion's skin and a cap, carrying a lyre, and explains that he has just returned from consulting Teiresias in Hades. The disguises had been assumed in order to enable him, if necessary, to pass, in the under-

[1] Pausanias, ix. 39, 5–14.

world, for Hercules, Odysseus,[1] or Orpheus, who had all successfully negotiated the descent in previous Greek literature, and were therefore known to those in authority. At first he pretends unwillingness to relate what he has seen, "lest," as he says, "I should have an information filed against myself for petty treason against Rhadamanthus."[2]

Menippus explains at some length what had driven him to seek the blind seer amongst the dead. Observing the glaring discrepancies between the morals of the gods (learnt from Homer and Hesiod) and the laws of men, he was thrown into great doubt and uncertainty. To which ought he to conform his own behaviour? Like the poet of Naishápúr, he applied to the philosophers, only to fall "out of the smoke into the fire." As a last resort he had sought out the Persian magus Mithrobarzanes, and induced him to conduct him, "on his own terms," to the infernal regions.

Menippus' account of his preliminary ceremonies and purifications is a most successful and amusing parody of Homer and Pausanias, but it must be passed over. The actual entrance to Hades is effected by the means which Odysseus employed, and in a similar place; a ditch is dug in a lonely wood, and the sheep are killed amidst vociferous

[1] The great traveller was supposed to wear a cap "quali utebantur viatores."

[2] The quotations are from the translation of Dr. Thomas Francklin (London, 1781).

incantations from the Persian. At once the earth was rent asunder, and the couple found themselves in the realms of the dead. Their coming was not unobserved; far from it; even Pluto "trembled in his dark abode." Plunging downwards through the fiery lake Pyriphlegethon, the travellers found Rhadamanthus "half dead with fear." Cerberus gave tongue, but Menippus struck his lyre, and "quickly lulled him to sleep with the sound." Then Charon mistook him for Hercules, and took him as a passenger "very willingly." The tribunal of Minos was found in active operation; the sinners were dragged towards him in groups, according to their offence. There is some little notion of making "the punishment fit the crime," as the rich and the usurers are "each weighed down with his yoke and crow of two talents about his neck."

Menippus, in another clever touch of parody, then describes a "new and most extraordinary species of orators," who appeared to accuse the dead. These were "the shadows of bodies made by the sun." They are specially reliable, because in life they have never left the body! The souls which Minos visited with greatest severity were those of men who, "puffed up by avarice and ambition," had expected little less than adoration amongst men. They stood before the judge naked,[1] stripped of all their wealth and rank, and Menippus describes the rather malicious pleasure which he himself took in accosting those he knew,

[1] Cf. the "Lay of Ishtar"; see above, p. 16, also p. 69.

and reminding them of their different state upon earth. "This discourse of mine," he says, "galled them most severely."

Leaving Minos, Menippus and his guide visit the place of punishment, where there is almost nothing that need detain us. Everything conforms to the classical tradition save the one statement that "the poor had half their punishment remitted, and, after intervals of rest, were again chastised for their misdemeanours." Lucian is quite noticeably sympathetic to the poor, and bitter against the rich.

Next, the Acherusian Mead, demigods and heroines, "with another crowd of ghosts, divided into nations and tribes, some old, withered, and, as Homer calls them, feeble ghosts. Others looked youthful and strong, particularly your Egyptian carcases, I suppose from the nature of their pickle."[1] The "ghosts" of this department are all skeletons, and therefore quite unrecognisable! Comment would be superfluous.

Menippus' reflections on what was revealed to him demand a passing reference. He compares human life to a public show, where Fortune lends the costumes to the actors, receiving them again when the show is over. The translator cites Shakespeare, as he is almost bound to, the parallel is so exact:

"Life . . . is a poor player,
Who struts and frets his hour upon the stage,
And then is heard no more, . . ."

---

[1] Readers will agree that eighteenth century English has its merits.

Philonides now asks if monuments and inscriptions are of no avail for the dead whom they commemorate. He is told that even Mausolus was "thrown into a little dark hole, amongst the common rabble," and only seemed very much oppressed by the weight of his tomb. Æacus allots to each his foot of space, rich and poor alike. "You would have smiled," continues Menippus, "to see some of our kings and satraps turned beggars there, . . . I could scarce contain myself when I saw Philip of Macedon there, as they pointed him out to me, in a corner, healing the wounds of old shoes."[1] Lucian must have a hit at Socrates, who was "walking about, and disputing with everybody, accompanied by Palamedes, Nestor, Ulysses, and all the old praters; his legs seemed to be swelled with the poisonous draught which he had taken."

Lucian's severity to the rich has been noticed. According to a decree passed during Menippus' sojourn in the lower world, their souls were condemned to inhabit generations of asses, "from ass to ass, five and twenty myriads of years, bearing burdens, and driven by the poor." When this decree had been read, "the magistrates gave their votes, the populace held up their hands, Proserpine howled her consent, and Cerberus barked; for thus, whatever is proposed here must be confirmed and made valid."

Now at length Menippus addresses Teiresias, and gets from him a word or two of very sound

[1] μισθοῦ ἀκούμενος τὰ σαπρὰ (σαθρὰ ?) τῶν ὑποδημάτων.

and practical advice, though neither in quantity nor quality does it appear to repay him for his long and arduous journey. Mithrobarzanes then despatches him "through a cranny," by a very short cut, into Bœotia.

CHAPTER III.

The "Descensus Christi."

The descent of our Lord into Hades is a subject which has never ceased to occupy the minds of men. The early Christian Fathers theorised upon it, denying the fact, or giving it each his own interpretation; and since their day there have not been wanting theologians to take up their mantle. The incident has laid hold of the imagination of artists and poets in many countries and centuries. Not five years ago we had a "Phantasy" on this very theme from the pen of one of our own most gifted and thoughtful dramatists.

The earliest authority for the descent is this passage from the First Epistle of St. Peter:[1] "Because Christ also suffered for sins once, the righteous for the unrighteous, that He might bring us to God; being put to death in the flesh, but quickened in the spirit; in which also He went and preached unto the spirits in prison, which aforetime were disobedient, when the longsuffering of God waited in the days of Noah, while the ark was a preparing." The statement is repeated later in the same letter:[2] "For unto this end was the

[1] Chap. iii. 18-20, R.V. [2] Chap. iv. 6.

gospel preached even unto the dead," . . . Possibly St. Paul[1] has the same idea in his mind when he writes: "Now this, 'He ascended,' what is it but that He also descended into the lower parts of the earth?" With these three passages from the canon we shall be content, though many other verses from both Testaments have been pressed — rather doubtfully — into the support of the fact.

As an element of the Messianic experience, St. Peter was familiar with the Descent into Hell from Jewish tradition. Of the prevalence of this there is the very strongest evidence. The Harrying of Hell is more than hinted at, prophetically of course, in the Talmud. Bigg, in his notes on the passage of St. Peter's Epistle,[2] quotes Weber, *Die Lehren des Talmud*,[3] where the necessary passages from the *Bereschit Rabba* are cited as follows: "Rabbi Joshua ben Levi spoke: 'I went with the angel Kippod, and there went with me Messias, the Son of David, until I came to the gates of Gehenna . . . But when those who are bound, who are in Gehenna, saw the light of the Messiah, they rejoiced to receive Him, and said: He will lead us out of this darkness.'" And again, from the same book: "This is that which stands written: 'We shall exult and rejoice in Thee. When? When the captives come up out of Hell, and the Shechinah at their head.'" The testimony of these passages is invaluable. They represent old oral traditions, and it is hard to think that these tradi-

[1] Eph. iv. 9.   [2] *Internat. Crit. Comm.*, p. 162.   [3] P. 351.

THE "DESCENSUS CHRISTI" 85

tions do not constitute the germ of the idea which St. Peter was the first to develop after it had taken shape in fact.

The Ethiopic Book of Enoch is hardly worth mentioning in this context. A vague and doubtful suggestion [1] of Christ's descent is spoiled by its association only with the fallen angels and not with the souls of men. There will be further occasion to refer to this unsatisfactory feature of *Enoch*, unsatisfactory, that is, from the present point of view. The verse reads as follows: "And there was great joy amongst them, and they blessed and glorified and extolled because the name of the Son of Man was revealed unto them."

At this point also may be transcribed a very brief mention of Christ's descent from *The Ascension of Isaiah*.[2] The third part of this apocalyptic work, the Vision of Isaiah, was probably written before the end of the first century.[3] Further use will be made of it in a succeeding chapter; meanwhile only three verses need be quoted, and these are taken from the note on the passage, as the MS. there translated seems preferable. "And He will descend into Hades, and make it and the phantoms of hell desolate. And He will seize the prince of death, and will plunder him, and will crush all his powers, and He will rise the third day, having certain righteous persons with Him . . ."[4] A

---

[1] lxix. 26, cited by Bigg, *loc. cit.* Dr. R. H. Charles, in his edition of *Enoch*, sub. v., simply says, "This is obscure."
[2] Ed. by R. H. Charles, D.D. [3] *Op. cit.*, p. xlv.
[4] *Op. cit.*, p. 62.

certain confusion is apparent between the Harrying of Hell and the Resurrection.

Next in order of time, probably, is a reference in the apocryphal *Gospel of St. Peter*, whose date Canon Armitage Robinson conjectures to be not much later than the middle of the second century. "And in the night in which the Lord's day was drawing on, as the soldiers kept watch two by two on guard, there was a great voice in the heaven; and they saw the heavens opened, and two men descending thence with great light and approaching the tomb. And that stone which was put at the door rolled away of itself and departed to one side; and the tomb was opened and both the young men entered in . . . Again they see coming forth from the tomb three men, and the two supporting the one, and a cross following them. And of the two the head reached unto the heaven, but the head of Him that was led by them overpassed the heavens. And they heard a voice from the heavens, saying, 'Hast Thou preached to them that sleep?' And an answer was heard from the Cross, 'Yea!'"[1] We have left behind the impressive simplicity of the canonical work, and find the new childish accessories anything but convincing.

Perhaps not many years later, according to Tischendorf's date, is the *Gospel of Nicodemus*, which contains the fullest extant description of Christ's visit to the dead. Dean Plumptre[2] draws

---

[1] §§ 9 and 10, p. 24 of Armitage Robinson's edition of the Gospel, (Cambridge University Press, 1892, 2nd edit.).

[2] *The Spirits in Prison.*

THE "DESCENSUS CHRISTI" 87

attention to the noticeable fact that this work is quite independent of those already mentioned, though, of course, dealing with the same tradition. The verses of St. Peter's Epistle are not once mentioned. The second part of this apocryphal Gospel consists of the written narrative of Karinus and Leucius, the sons of Simeon, who had risen with Christ, and remained on this earth only such time as was necessary to complete their revelation. Each wrote his story separately, and the two were afterwards found to tally exactly, letter for letter.

The narrative thus obtained is long and circumstantial: the chief persons of the drama are Hades or Tartarus (the prince of hell), Satan, Adam, Seth, Enoch, David, Elijah, Isaiah, Simeon, and the penitent thief. Only the briefest sketch of the incident can be given in this place. Passing over Hades' recriminations of Satan, and his curious reference to Lazarus, we come to the "Voice as of thunders, and the shouting of spirits: 'Lift up your gates, ye princes; and be ye lifted up, ye everlasting gates; and the King of Glory shall come in.'"[1] Hades now thrusts Satan out of his dominions, shuts his "cruel gates of brass," and fixes his iron bars. The saints expostulate, and David and Isaiah exult in the verification of the prophecies which they had uttered in the body. And then, "there came to Hades in the form of a man, the Lord of Majesty, and lighted up the eternal darkness, and burst asunder the indissoluble chains;

[1] The quotations are from Walker's translation (Ante-Nicene Christian Library, vol. xvi.).

and the aid of unconquered power visited us, sitting in the profound darkness of Transgressions, and in the shadow of death of sins." It is this sublime moment that Dürer's genius has fixed for ever in no less than three great works of art.

All hell trembles at Christ's coming. His first act is to deliver Satan to the power of Hades, who renews his reproaches upon the "prince of perdition, . . . Beelzebub, derision of angels," who had brought to his realms " one innocent and just, and (thereby) lost the guilty, the impious, and the unjust of the whole world." To this Christ adds his doom: Satan is to be in Hades' power for ever, in place of Adam and his sons, Christ's just ones. The Saviour then proceeds with His work of redemption: "Come to Me," He says, stretching forth His hand, "all My saints, who have My image and likeness." He holds Adam by the right hand and greets him, "Peace be to thee, with all thy children, My righteous ones." Then, making the sign of the cross upon all of them, He leads His saints to heaven, and delivers them to Michael the Archangel.

In Paradise the saints meet two men, "Ancient of Days," Enoch and Elijah, who had of old been caught up to heaven. These, it appears, are the "two witnesses" of the strange passage in the Revelation of St. John.[1] Here, too, the saints listen to the story of the repentant thief, who has already been placed "on the right of Paradise," on exhibiting to the angel the sign of the cross on his

[1] Chap. xi. 3-13.

shoulders, the token of his Redeemer's promise. "More of the other mysteries of God" Karinus and Leucius are not permitted to reveal.

But it is time, now that we have a full statement of the tradition, to pause for a moment and consider what it means. The fact of Christ's descent is one of the main tenets of our own belief—"He descended into Hell"—though this Article took some centuries to assure its place in the Apostles' Creed. But the nature and object of Christ's sojourn with the dead, it is upon these that diverse views have been and are held, and that it is now time for something to be said. We are obviously not concerned to refute the arguments of those who deny the whole episode, and explain otherwise the verses in the Epistles of St. Peter and St. Paul.

The now almost universally accepted exegesis of St. Peter's passage is one which is substantiated by the story of Karinus and Leucius, namely, that Christ's mission in the underworld was to liberate from Hades, or the intermediate state, and to take with Him to Paradise the souls of those who, born before His time, had had no chance of His redemption. It seems best to interpret the special mention of the generation of Noah in either of the two following ways.[1] Peter says, "even"[2] to them, types of wickedness, and by implication, therefore, to all others; or possibly he had in his mind the two great periods of the

[1] As in an unpublished lecture on the passage by Professor Marcus Dods.
[2] καὶ τοῖς κ.τ.λ.

world's history—the prehistoric period, which had been ended by the Flood, and the later post-diluvian ages, which he believed were soon to be ended, not by water, but by fire. Either of these explanations seems to make his reference to Noah natural and easy.

But countless commentators, from the days of the Fathers[1] onwards, have held that Christ's mission means far more than this, and that we are bound, in fairness to ourselves and in justice to His mercy, to extend still further the implication of the facts. "We have no sufficient ground," says Plumptre, "for limiting the work on which (the Apostle) dwells to the representative instance or the time-boundaries of which he speaks." The same writer's deductions from the words of our Lord Himself are impressive; and his conclusion, shared in these days by so many, is that Death does not put a final stop to the progress of the soul and to its reconciliation with God,—in short, that, save such as are absolutely hardened in sins, for whom the further chance would be unavailing, all the dead are "prisoners of hope." For ages Protestant thinkers have been deterred from this doctrine by its resemblance to the Catholic purgatory, and its consequent participation in the dangers and abuses of that belief. The subject is one upon which it is ridiculous to dogmatise, difficult even to hold a decided view. Of the theory of the "wider hope" we can only say, then, that it is a beautiful and a

[1] Huidekopfer collects the beliefs of the first three centuries in his book, *Christ's Mission to the Underworld*.

comfortable doctrine, but that it is impossible to show convincing scriptural authority for it in view of the conflicting statements of the New Testament, and that it is equally impossible to assert that it is the *necessary* logical conclusion from our human intuitions.

To return to the literature of the "Descensus Christi," we first find another apocryphal work referring to the episode. In the *Anaphora Pilati*[1] the Roman procurator reports that after the Crucifixion many of the dead had risen, whom "the Jews themselves" witnessed to be Abraham, Isaac, Jacob, and others of the saints. "And there were very many," he adds, "whom I also saw appearing in the body." "And as lightnings come suddenly in winter, so majestic men appeared in glorious robes, an innumerable multitude, whose voice was heard as that of a very great thunder, crying out: 'Jesus that was crucified is risen: come up out of Hades, ye that have been enslaved in the underground regions of Hades.'"

Wherever Christianity went, the story, as we have already remarked, impressed itself deeply upon the imaginations of men, and it will be sufficient illustration of this to show how the "Descensus Christi" first made its appearance in our own language and country. Amongst the poems connected with the name of Cædmon, which range from the end of the seventh to the end of the ninth century, there is nothing from the pen of the founder of

[1] First Greek form (Ante-Nicene Christian Library, vol. xvi.).

the school himself which deals with the subject. To his most noted follower, however, are attributed two poems which treat of the Descent.[1] The second part of Cynewulf's *Crist* has for its subject the Ascension, and after describing the actual event, the poet reverts to the Harrying of Hell in a fine passage:[2]

> "It is well spoken, as the Scripture saith,
> That radiant angels at that holy tide,
> Descending in the clouds in legion came
> To meet Him; . . .
>
> . . . .
>
> Now hath the Holy One despoiled hell
> Of all the tribute that in ancient days
> It basely forged within that home of strife.
> Now are they quelled, the devil's champions,
> In living torture humbled and held bound,
> Bereft of prowess, down in hell's abyss;
> The gruesome foes might not in battle speed
> With weapon-thrusts, when He, the King of Glory,
> The Helm of heaven's realm, waged warfare there
> Against His ancient foes with His sole might.
> Then drew He forth from durance the best spoil,
> A folk unnumbered, from the burgh of fiends,
> This very band which ye here gaze upon.
>
> . . . .
>
> . . . Open, O ye gates!
> The Lord of all, the King, creation's Source,
> Will lead through you unto the Citadel,
> Unto the joy of joys, with host not small,
> The folk which from the devils He hath reft
> By His own victory."

---

[1] Stopford Brooke, *English Literature from the Beginning to the Norman Conquest*, pp. 170, 172, and 186.

[2] Gollancz's translation, ll. 545 *seq*. About a dozen lines are omitted in order to shorten the quotation.

THE "DESCENSUS CHRISTI" 93

Later in the same part of the poem[1] there is a second reference to the Descent, which deserves to be noted for its quaint fancy. The poet quotes, if his liberal transcription can be called quoting, these words from the Song of Solomon:[2] "He cometh leaping upon the mountains, skipping upon the hills." The ensuing commentary is almost grotesque: under the figure of a "leap" is presented each of the six outstanding events in the life of Christ. A very short quotation will suffice to show the nature of the passage:

> "The first leap was, when He came to the damsel,
> The spotless maid, and sinlessly took there
> A human form, . . ."

and so His birth, His crucifixion, and His burial:

> . . . "The fifth leap was,
> When He bowed down the multitude of hell
> In living torment, and bound their king within,
> The devil's advocate, so grim of mood,
> With fiery fetters, where he lieth yet,
> Fastened in prison there with manacles,
> And shackled with his sins."

Authorities are almost unanimous in ascribing also to Cynewulf a "Descent into Hell," written soon after the middle of the eighth century. This poem, the text of which is in a rather imperfect condition, forms part of the *Exeter Book*, the MS. left to his Cathedral by Leofric, the first Bishop of Exeter, in the year 1046.[3] In matter and style it is very

---

[1] ll. 710-742.   [2] Chap. ii. 8.
[3] Benjamin Thorpe's *Exeter Book* (London, 1842), Preface. From this translation the quotations are taken.

similar to the other poems of this period to which we refer. One or two short selections, therefore, will suffice to convey some idea of the work. When the "noble women" go to Christ's tomb before dawn, we read, "open was that earth-house; the Noble's corse had received life's spirit; earth trembled, laughed hell's inmates; men awoke exulting from earth, Majesty arose triumphant and sagacious."

Considerable importance is attached to the figure of St. John the Baptist, in fact a large part of the poem is put into his mouth. Though he does not say so in explicit terms (very possibly owing to a lacuna in the MS.[1]), it is quite fair to infer that St. John's work of heralding Christ did not cease at his death. We shall presently have occasion to refer to another work in which St. John arrogates to himself the same function in Hades. The Baptist naturally apostrophises the Jordan, and thereby imparts an additional touch of poetry to the work.

After some of the usual Old Testament saints have been mentioned by name as being delivered from hell, the following enumeration is perhaps worth quoting:—". . . patriarchs many: so also a company of men, a host of prophets, a band of women, many damsels, people numberless." One further extract will be enough: it includes four lines of quite picturesque description. "Saw then John the Victor Child of God with that kingly pomp come to hell; perceived then the sad in

[1] Thorpe, *op. cit.*, p. 460, l. 36, and p. 461, l. 1.

THE "DESCENSUS CHRISTI" 95

mind God Himself's journey: he saw hell's door serenely shine, which long before had been lock'd, with darkness deck'd: joyful was the thane."

There remains still one other version of the Harrying of Hell in the Cædmonian poems. This is taken from the second half of the MS. which Junius left to the Bodleian Library,[1] and is therefore translated by Benjamin Thorpe in his edition of *Cædmon's Metrical Paraphrase*. The latter half of the Junian MS. was called "Christ and Satan," and consists of three poems, "The Fallen Angels" (a sort of Paradise Lost), "The Harrowing of Hell," and "The Temptation."[2] The date is in the neighbourhood of the year 900.[3] "Anguish came on Hell, and thunder crash at dawn of day, before the Judge when he shattered the gates of hell. 'Terrible is this,' cry the friends, wailing far and wide through the windy hall, 'since this storm has come on us, the Hero with His following, the Lord of Angels. Before Him shines a lovelier light, never seen since we were on high among the heavenly host.'"[4] The "blessed souls, the race of Adam," then ascend to Paradise, but Eve may not behold its glories until she has repeated the story of the Fall. There follows a fine descriptive touch, when all the souls raise themselves upon their elbows from their prostrate positions: "though hell's horror dreadful seemed, they were all for this glad

---

[1] Stopford Brooke, *op. cit.*, p. 242.
[2] *Ibid.*, p. 248.   [3] *Ibid.*, p. 242.
[4] This is Brooke's version, which we quote in preference to the bald line-for-line translation of Thorpe.

in their sufferings . . . that their Lord would for their help seek hell."[1] Christ then thrusts the fiends deeper into "hell's hot abyss," and conducts the saints to Paradise. The remainder of the poem is taken up first with His discourse to the saints, and then with His Resurrection and other like matters.

Finally, before leaving the "Descensus Christi" altogether, room must be found for an example of the dramatic treatment of the subject, the growth, as an authority conjectures, of seed sown by the dialogue passages of the Cædmonian poems. The miracle-play, from which a few lines will presently be transcribed, is perhaps actually a year or two more recent than the limit of the present inquiry, but it dates from the fourteenth century, and can justify its insertion here on other grounds. It is the oldest drama in the English language, and, besides, it is a type of many still older in other tongues and conceivably in our own. The learned editor of the play, James Orchard Halliwell, remarks of the legend of Christ's descent, that "it forms one of almost every known series of miracle-plays, generally under the title of the 'Harrowing of Hell.'"[2] (It may be incidentally remarked that the word "harrowing"[3] is an obsolete by-form of "harrying," from the perfectly familiar verb to "harry,"—a bird's nest, for instance.)

---

[1] Thorpe, *op. cit.*, pp. 291, 292. There is a small hiatus in the passage quoted.

[2] The *Harrowing of Hell*, a miracle-play, etc. etc., ed. by James Orchard Halliwell (London 1840), Intr. p. 7.

[3] See Murray's *New English Dictionary*.

THE "DESCENSUS CHRISTI"

The miracle-play opens with a prologue as follows:[1]—

"Alle herkneth to me nou!
A strif wolle y tellen ou
Of Jhesu ant of Sathan, —
Tho[2] Jhesu wes to helle y-gan
Forte vacche thenne[3] hys,
Ant bringen hem to parays.
The Devel hevede so muche pousté,[4]
That alle mosten to helle te;[5]
Nas non[6] so holy prophete
Seththe[7] Adam and Eve then appel ete,
Ant he were at this worldes fyne,
That he ne moste to helle pyne;[8]
Ne shulde he never thenne come
Nere[9] Jhesu Christ, Godes sone."

After some thirty lines omitted, the prologue ends thus:

"Tho Jhesu hevede shed ys blod,
For our neode,[10] upon the rod;[11]
In Godhead toke he then way
That to helle gates lay;
The[12] he com there, tho[13] seide he
Asse i shal nouthe[14] telle the."

Christ now enters and recounts His sufferings. At line 57 He begins to announce His intention:

"Adam! thou havest aboht[15] sore,—
I nul soffre[16] that no more;

---

[1] The original is quoted, but not as a reflection on Halliwell's excellent translation.

[2] When. [3] Fetch thence. [4] Power.
[5] Had to go to hell. [6] There was no. [7] Since.
[8] Hell's pain. [9] Were it not for . . . [10] Need.
[11] Cross. [12] When. [13] Then.
[14] Now. [15] Paid. [16] Will not suffer.

> Adam! thou hast duere[1] aboht
> That thou levedst[2] me noht
> Y shal the bringe of helle pyne,
> Ant with the alle myne."

At this point Satan enters, and the manner of his speech is some index of the taste of the age which produced the play:

> "Who is that ich here there?
> Ich him rede[3] spake na more,
> For he may so muche do
> That he shal us come to,
> Forte buen[4] oure fere,[5]
> Ant fouden[6] how we pleyen[7] here."

This might serve, as illustration of the "miserable doggerel" of the altercation between Satan and Christ, but it is hard to refrain from quoting one especially ludicrous passage. Satan argues,

> "Whoso buyth any thyng,
> Hit is his ant his ofspryng:
> Adam hungry com me to,—
> Monrade dude y him me do.[8]
> For an appel ich gef[9] hym,
> He is myn ant al hys kun."[10]

The following answer is put in the mouth of Christ:

> "Sathanas! hit wes myn,—
> The appel that thou geve hym;
> The appel ant the appel tre,
> Bothe were maked throurh me.

---

[1] Dearly.   [2] Believedst.   [3] Advise.
[4] Be.   [5] Companion.   [6] Find out.
[7] Amuse ourselves.   [8] Homage made I him to me do.
[9] Gave.   [10] Kin.

THE "DESCENSUS CHRISTI"

> Hou myhtest thou, on eny wyse
> Of other monnes thyng make marchandise?
> Seththe he wes boht wyth myn,
> Wyth resoun wolle ich haven hym."

Christ presently commands the gates of hell to be opened; the "Janitor" fears and flees, and Christ bursts down the gates, and enters to meet His saints:

> "Helle gates wolle y falle,
> Ant out taken myne alle.
> Sathanas, y bynde the, her shalt thou lay,
> O that[1] come domesday."

Adam, Eve, Abraham, David, John the Baptist, and Moses in turn greet their Saviour, and the play ends with an Epilogue of ten lines, a prayer for grace to avoid the pain of hell. Only one point calls for special remark, and it has been recently remarked in connection with Cynewulf's "Descent into Hell." John the Baptist proclaims himself as even in hell the forerunner of Christ, a statement which reminds us of the similar function allotted to Judas Iscariot in the Cædmonian poem,[2] and of the common belief of the Fathers that the Old Testament saints were sent to Hades, that is to abide in the intermediate state, for the same purpose.

The absolute and childish simplicity of the play is its most marked characteristic. Often this inclines to the grotesque, but it occasionally achieves some beauty and pathos.

[1] Until. [2] Thorpe, *op. cit*.

> "Adam, ich have geve mi lyf
> For the ant for Eve thi wyf.
> Wendest[1] thou ich were ded for noht?
> For my deth wes monkune[2] y-boht."

As a conclusion to the subject, it will be well to transcribe the lines from the *Inferno*,[3] which contains Dante's reference. Filled with pity for the great souls whom he finds confined in the limbus, or first circle, of hell, he asks his guide:

> "Did ever any by his merits go,
> Or by another's, hence, and then was blest?"

Vergil makes answer in the following lines:

> " . . . I was but a new-come guest,
> When here I saw a Mighty One[4] descend,
> And on His brow the conqueror's crown did rest;
> He bade our first sire's spirit with him wend,
> Abel, his son, and Noah too did bring,
> Moses, lawgiver, loyal to the end,
> Abraham the Patriarch, David, too, the king,
> Israel, with all his children, and his sire,
> Rachael, for whom he bore such suffering,
> And others, whom He placed in heaven's blest choir;
> And thou should'st know that human spirits none
> Gained before these salvation's joy entire."

---

[1] Thinkest.   [2] Mankind.
[3] Canto iv. l. 49 (Plumptre's trans.).
[4] Dante never uses the name of Christ in hell.

CHAPTER IV.

APOCRYPHAL LITERATURE.

It will not escape notice that a quite definite and solitary chapter in the history of visits to the dead has been closed. Christ's descent was in the nature of the case unique; it alone resulted in any change in the underworld, no other visit [1] was productive of the slightest alteration in the state of the dead as a whole, though we do observe one or two cases of successful intercession for individual sinners. In short, the "Descensus Christi" was a revolutionary incident, not a vision, and in resuming the thread of our history we return to this latter class of story.

Nor do we find a very marked increase of spirituality in the legends. There is, of course, the general broad difference in environment and accessories which is the inevitable result of Christian authorship, but we do not discover, nor could we, that the human race has leaped at a bound to a highly spiritual conception of a future state. In the first blush of the Christian faith, indeed, as represented by the writings of the apostles and

[1] With the exception of the fanciful episode in the *Apocalypse of Paul*, and the feeble imitation of it in the *Apocalypse of the Virgin Mary*.

of the very early Christians, there is trace of such a movement. But the second century is marked by a pronounced retrogression, and the literature of our subject partakes of its character. As an illustration of the materialism which still hangs over the Christian stories, it will be noticed that the narrators cling with the same tenacity to descriptions of the torments of hell: it is in these graphic passages that they are felt to be in their element. The Christian writer, apart from the obvious difference of setting above noticed, is not very far ahead of his pagan brother in realising the joys of Paradise.

There is, of course, one work of which this statement is especially far from true, the earliest Christian apocalypse, the "Revelation" of St. John the Divine. Nothing could be much further removed from some of the pagan legends to which reference has been made, but it is also true that St. John differs almost as much from his contemporaries and successors in the same field of literature. Even his subject is hardly the same, and his treatment is on quite another level of exaltation. No apology is therefore necessary for abstaining from any analysis of the Book of Revelation, about which, except by way of occasional reference, we shall have nothing further to say.

Hebrew Visions.

It is not possible yet, however, to proceed to an account of the Christian apocalypses. To do so at once would be to omit an extremely important branch of the literature of the subject. This will be easily understood if it be for a moment considered what the sources were from which the early Christian writers drew. The classical legends and the classical literature doubtless played their part, but unquestionably an even more important influence ought to be attributed to the traditions and writings of the Jews. That the authors of the early Christian apocalypses were familiar with this set of traditions their very names imply, and little doubt will be left on the question after a perusal of the works of which mention is now to be made.

In the *Journal of the Royal Asiatic Society* for 1893, Dr. Gaster published translations of no less than eight manuscripts of this class, and to his article we are indebted for what follows. Dr. Gaster argues a pre-Christian date for these works, from the existence of almost identical Christian visions, such as the apocalypses of Peter and Paul; his opinion, however, is not shared by most critics. Whether the visions were committed to writing before the Christian era or not, the conclusion is probably true as to the traditions, and the likelihood is that the descriptions of heaven and hell, of which abstracts are now to be given, have, through the medium of the apocalypses of Peter and Paul and their compeers and successors, exercised an influence upon the whole literature of the subject which it would be hard to exaggerate.

The Revelation of Moses.

The title *Revelation of Moses* serves to distinguish Dr. Gaster's first Hebrew vision from the Greek *Apocalypse of Moses*,[1] which is a totally different work. The *Revelation* is of some length, being divided into sixty-eight sections, and, as will usually be the case, those sections which concern hell yield far more relevant information than those which attempt to describe heaven.

The occasion of Moses' visit to the dead is as follows. When he demurs at being sent to deliver the children of Israel, God answers that he has humbled himself in saying, "Who am I that I should go unto Pharaoh?" but that He will honour him. He accordingly sends the angel of His presence to bring Moses before Him. Before he may behold the angels, Moses' flesh has to be turned into fire; he is then carried up to heaven by a vast escort of angels.

The angel of the presence proceeds to conduct Moses through heavens seven in number, corresponding, in this vision, to the days of the week. The sevenfold division will be found to be of frequent recurrence, and at this first mention of it a word of comment may not be out of place. For the origin of the elementary idea it is necessary to cast back many centuries: it will be remembered how the Babylonian Ishtar descended through seven gates to hell, and that the Egyptian hell visited by the son of Rameses II. consisted

[1] Tischendorf, *Apocal. Apocr.* (Lips. 1866), p. 1.

of seven departments. Later, in the Greek and Latin classical authors, a similar though not identical division was observed in the spheres. Its use in an everyday phrase of our own language is sufficient testimony to the popularity of the conception.

The first heaven seen by Moses is full of windows, at each of which stands an angel. A somewhat lengthy catalogue of the windows is given: "the window of prayer, . . . the window of crying, the window of joy, . . . the window of satiation, the window of famine," and so forth.

There is nothing to detain us until Moses reaches the fifth heaven, which is inhabited by a rather curious sort of angel, "half of fire and half of snow, and the snow is above the fire without extinguishing it." The explanation offered is this: "for God makes peace between them, as it is said, 'He maketh peace in His high places.'" There is one very close resemblance to a passage in the Book of Isaiah, a picture of the angels with six wings which stand before God. The representation of the angel of death is curious, whom Moses finds on the point of departing to fetch the soul of "Job the pious." "His countenance was totally different from those of the other angels, for he was ugly and his height of 540 years' journey, and he was girded forty times round his waist. From the sole of the foot unto the head he was full of fiery eyes, and whosoever looked at him fell down in dread." The narrative continues as we should expect: "And Moses said before God, 'May it be Thy will, O Lord my God, God of my fathers, that Thou shouldst not deliver me into the hands of this angel.'" There is a certain sort of interest in the account of the heavens; it abounds with these monstrous and absurd descriptions of angels, but it is almost destitute of eschatological significance.

The angel Gabriel was now commissioned to guide the "beloved servant" Moses through hell. Moses was reassured of his personal safety, and when he entered "the fire of hell withdrew for 500 parasangs."

The catalogue of punishment and crime which follows is lengthy and in parts extremely unsavoury. Criminals are suspended in fire by all the different members with which they had offended. A short abstract will suffice both to give an idea of the vision and to exhibit the indebtedness of the later Christian apocalypses.

Hanging by their eyes or their tongues are those whose eyes have in life been filled with lust or avarice.

Adulterers, thieves, and murderers are also suspended, with their hands tied.

Other men hanging by ear or tongue "neglected the study of the law, and talked slander and vain words."

Women hang by their breasts, or by their hair, who have immodestly exposed these to view.

Hell is represented as insatiable, crying for sinners that it may destroy them. A somewhat fuller quotation of one or two sections will show how grotesque the composition occasionally is.

"Moses went further, and saw two sinners hanged by their feet with their heads downwards, and they cried by reason of the torture of hell, and their bodies were covered with black worms, each worm 500 parasangs long." These sinners long for death, which will not come to them. Their crimes were perjury, Sabbath-breaking, intellectual pride, uncharitableness, and other similar offences.

"Moses went then to another place. There the sinners were lying on their faces; and he saw two thousand scorpions swarming over them and stinging them and torturing them, and the sinners cried bitterly. Each scorpion has 70,000 mouths, and each mouth 70,000 stings, and each sting has 70,000 vesicles filled with poison and venom, and with these are the sinners imbued and thus are they tortured, and their eyes are sunk in their sockets for fear and dread." The offences of these unfortunates are not nearly so heinous as a proper sense of proportion would expect. They may be quoted as a type of the curious and far-reaching selection of crimes in which this vision indulges. "These have wasted the money of others; they have taken bribery, and elevated themselves above others; they have put their neighbours publicly to shame; they have delivered up their brother Israelite to the Gentile; they have denied the oral law, and maintained that God did not create the world." This list indicates a high standard of morality, as we should expect; it also gives very ancient witness to the "clan" spirit of the Hebrew, which has since become proverbial; but, in connection with the torment just quoted, it betokens a want of fairness and reserve. Justice demands a finer graduation of penalty, but the present author seems to expend upon each pit of hell the worst that his by no means sterile imagination can devise.

It is unnecessary to multiply instances of this sort. A bare mention, therefore, must suffice for the knee-deep pit of "miry clay," where the wretched victims have their teeth broken with fiery stones from morning till evening, and prolonged again during the night "to the length of a parasang," in order to be broken anew on the following day. The last chastisement which Moses witnessed deserves a fuller report. Here "the wicked were punished by fire, being half in fire and half in snow, with worms crawling up and down their bodies, and a fiery collar round their necks, and having no rest, except on Sabbath days and festival days. All the other days they are tortured in hell." Such is the penalty of adultery, sodomy, idolatry, and murder, and here, too, are those who have cursed their parents. These lines are full of interest. In the first place, this is the first occurrence in these pages [1] of cold as a means of torment in hell. This feature is commoner in the literature of northern countries, where ice and snow were more bitter foes than fire, and has frequently been the subject of remark in connection with Scandinavian legends. The respite of the

[1] With the exception of a slight mention in the story of Thespesius, v. p. 70.

souls on Sundays and feast days also calls for remark; the author of *The Apocalypse of Paul* not only repeats this, but explains it in a manner which redounds to the great glory of the apostle.

With one further quotation the account of hell may be closed. "God said to Moses: 'Moses, My servant, I have created two parks: Paradise and Hell. Whosoever committeth evil deeds goeth down to Hell, and whosoever doth good deeds cometh into Paradise.'"

Gabriel then leads Moses to Paradise, which must be regarded as belonging somewhere to the scheme of the seven heavens, though its situation is not described. It is the abode of the just, the "reward of the pious," and more interesting than the fabulous heavens of which an account has been given. It is perhaps worth notice that both here and in hell Moses' advent is the cause of remark. "Not here is thy place," says the Lord of Hell, while the angels are surprised at his premature arrival. "Thy time is not yet arrived to leave the world," is their greeting. The leading features of Paradise may be briefly collected. The Tree of Life grows here, and there is altogether a very distinct flavour of the New Testament apocalypse. Moses can hardly have been the borrower. A short quotation will illustrate this resemblance.

"Moses looked up and saw seventy thrones fixed, one next to another; all made of precious stones, or emerald, sapphire and diamond and precious pearls, and the foot of each was of gold and fine gold. Around each throne stood seventy angels."

The largest and most important throne is for Abraham; the thrones of other saints vary, "each after his worth and position and the good works he hath performed in the world." On thrones of pearls are seated "the scholars who study the law day and night for the sake of heaven." The pious are enthroned in precious stones, the just in rubies, the repentant in gold, and, curiously enough, there is a throne of copper for wicked men who through the merits of pious sons obtain "a portion of heavenly bliss." As an instance of this class, Terah, the father of Abraham, is mentioned, "who had worshipped all the idols in the world."

There remains only one section which deserves notice, and this it will be advisable to quote in full, as it has either been very much copied or embodies a very popular set of ideas.

"Afterwards Moses looked down, and beheld a spring of living water welling forth from underneath the tree of life and dividing itself into four streams, and it comes from under the throne of glory, and they encompass the Paradise from one end to the other. And under each throne there flow four rivers, one of honey, the second of milk, the third of wine, and the fourth of pure balsam. These all pass beneath the feet of the just, who are seated upon thrones."

There are two recensions of this apocalypse, but, after the first, there is not much in the second over which it seems advisable to pause. It is very much shorter than the other, consisting only of nine sections, most of them of only a few lines.

APOCRYPHAL LITERATURE

It contains, however, one important conception, which is also to be found in the Talmud (Moses is himself the narrator in this version):—" I saw further the fiery river Rigyon, which comes out before God, from under the throne of Glory, and is formed from the perspiration of the holy Creatures who support the throne of Glory, and out of dread of God's majesty perspire fire. . . . The Almighty sits and judges the ministering angels, and after the judgment they bathe in that river of fire and are renewed. Afterwards the river flows on and carries with it fiery coals, and falls on the heads of the sinners in hell." Such an account of the origin of the fiery river which so constantly recurs throughout our literature is not without interest.

The Revelation of Rabbi Joshua ben Levi.

Though *The Revelation of Moses* seems unquestionably to be the fountainhead of future inspiration, there are many points in the other visions which Dr. Gaster translates which have left their mark on later writings. There are two accounts of a vision of Rabbi Joshua, each of which contains important eschatological features. Want of space forbids a narration of the fantastic manner in which the Rabbi takes Paradise by storm, but immediately following this is a passage of possible significance. When Rabbi Joshua swears by the name of God that he will not leave Paradise, having once effected an entrance, the ministering angels are sent to inquire if he has ever broken an oath upon earth; for the verdict of God is that if that be so, "then shall this oath of his be likewise void and null."

Of Rabbi Joshua's Paradise it is not necessary to say much. It is divided, however, again into "seven compartments," each, it may be added, a square of twelve myriads of miles. The gorgeous furnishing and decoration of some of these is paralleled in later times. In these compartments are various classes of people, but it would be a mere waste of time to catalogue them. The classification appears to be as nearly as possible devoid of ethical meaning, though it is full of rampant Judaism. For instance, in reply to a question concerning the third heaven, if no preparations are made there to receive Gentiles, the Rabbi is informed that "the Almighty gives the reward of every good deed they do in their lifetime, but after death they go down to hell; whilst the sinners in Israel get their punishment in their lifetime in that world, but after death they obtain the merit of their good deeds here." The height of the absurdity is reached when the Rabbi solemnly quotes as comment, and as it were authority, these three words of a previous father of his Church—"And he payeth." Again, the Messiah, the son of David, is found in the fifth heaven, while the seventh is occupied by "those who had died from illnesses caused through the sins of Israel." Besides being obscure, such a classification is felt to be in the highest degree random and unsatisfactory.

To pass to the account of hell, the first, and, indeed, the only point of interest is the suggestion of the Messianic deliverance of souls, which has been quoted above in the chapter which deals with the "Descensus Christi." For the rest, the Rabbi's hell consists of departments measuring ten miles by five, in which ten nations of the Gentiles are driven by angels armed with staves into pits of fire. The souls come out of the fire as if it had never touched them, but are immediately thrust in again. Absalom presides, and he alone is exempted from punishment, and honoured "with the honour of a king," because he is a Hebrew and the son of David. Clearly there is nothing new or important here.

Of *The Revelation of Rabbi Joshua* there are likewise two versions, and as they vary very considerably, a brief review of the other must now be given. Paradise has two gates, and the same four rivers as were seen by Moses, with the difference that here they flow through the city, and not round it. The just are received by angels who divest them of their burial clothes and robe them in "eight clothes, woven out of clouds of glory," and other accoutrements, similarly gorgeous and similarly meaningless. They undergo, however, three transformations in three "wards" of Paradise, which are more suggestive. In the first they become children and enjoy the pleasures of childhood, after which they pass successively through the wards of youth and mature age.

The description of the trees of Paradise is striking, and will find echoes in Christian apocalyptic writings. This is specially true of the tree of life, which has five hundred different tastes and perfumes. "Over it hang seven clouds of glory, and the winds blow from all the four corners and waft its many odours from one end of the world to the other."

The Rabbi finds, in this version also, seven compartments of the just in Paradise. In the first are martyrs, in the second "those who were drowned," in the third "Rabbi Johanan and his disciples!" The list ends rather more happily. The fifth group are penitents, the sixth "children who have not yet tasted sin in their lives," and the seventh the poor, who, in spite of their poverty, have studied the law and the Talmud and "acquired moral life." The children of this catalogue (which cannot be regarded as a graduated classification) are especially interesting in view of the various treatment of unbaptized infants of which a brief account has been given in a previous chapter.

Minor Visions.

The limits of our immediate subject have from the beginning imposed a rule upon our selection of material which now again comes into operation. General views concerning the future state are in these pages irrelevant; and in accordance with this principle we must now pass over many sections of homily, as being without the scope of our subject, and select from Dr. Gaster's translations only such passages as are written distinctly in the vision form, and are therefore entitled to a place amongst visits to the Dead.

First, then, a short vision of the same Rabbi Joshua, in which Elijah shows him the chastisements of hell, and in which the same set of traditions is drawn upon as in *The Revelation of Moses*, or, possibly, one author has directly copied the other. The whole vision consists of a catalogue of crimes and their chastisements. Men were hanging by their hair who had "let their hair grow to adorn themselves for sin"; they were suspended by their eyes if they had "followed their eyes to sin"; by their noses when they had "perfumed themselves to sin." Slanderers were hung up by the tongue, robbers by their hands, and so on, in the usual style of appropriateness, of which we have by now had copious illustration, and which we are again destined to meet. Fire, worms, and snow are the familiar instruments of torture, but there are one or two new details. Blasphemers are fed on fiery coals. Those who ate on fast-days are now forced to eat "bitter gall." Others are forced to eat fine sand, which breaks their teeth: these were robbers, and the detail of the chastisement will recall the similar but grotesque passage of Moses' Revelation.

In the course of the homily on hell in which the above vision is related, Rabbi Johanan makes this remark: "There are five punishments in hell, and Isaiah saw them all." Only in the first of these is there anything at all new. "He entered the first compartment, and saw there two men carrying pails full of water on their shoulders, and they pour that water into a pit, which, however, never fills." These are the covetous, but it is not the congruity of their chastisement that is remarkable, but the nature of the penalty itself. It is so different from the usual "fire and worms," that it is hard not to think that the famous Greek story has been made use of. The other four modes of torture are quite negligible, except, of course, that they tend to add to the permanence of the details which they repeat.

There is still another vision connected with the name of Rabbi Joshua ben Levi, but very few words will describe it. The Rabbi took measurements of the first compartment of the seven into which this vision divides hell, but his figures are not even amusing. The punishment is the same in all the divisions, and is executed in pits by lions. When the sinners have been devoured by these, their bones are thrown into a fire. Each compartment (except the first) has its president, as before, immune from punishment, and, besides, a punishing angel. The presidents are Hebrews, and, by implication, the damned are, as above, the Gentiles. All this is quite unimportant; but the final lines of the vision present a feature foreign to most other works of the period, though soon to reappear. "This is the punishment of the tens of thousands who are in each compartment, and they do not see each other, for it is dark, and this darkness is that deep darkness which existed before the world was created."

The final vision of Dr. Gaster's group is not here relevant. It is a vision of Paradise of a sort, but the interpretation of Paradise is so very one-sided, that as a matter of fact the vision only tells of the misfortunes and subsequent glories which are in store for the Children of Israel.

The Books of Enoch.

It has been thought proper to head the list of Hebrew Revelations with that of Moses, on account of its paramount importance in the evolution of those theories of retribution and reward after death which are the most immediate object of the present inquiry. It must not be thought, therefore, that this order has been determined on chronological grounds. Experts find it impossible, indeed, to fix accurately the dates of many works of this period; and it may well be that, in the present case, an anachronism is committed; but an exact chronological order, within a group such as is now under examination, is beside the point. The question is not whether Enoch borrowed from Moses, but what both handed down to a later period. We have already had occasion to quote *The Ethiopic Book of Enoch* in connection with the "Descensus Christi." Though the work is largely of a prophetic nature, and therefore not so directly interesting, it contains points too important to let slip. Further, it must be noticed that there are two books connected with the name of Enoch,—*The Book of Enoch* and *The Book of the Secrets of Enoch*,—

which will be referred to as the *Ethiopic* and the *Slavonic*[1] respectively.

The Ethiopic Enoch,[2] which Dr. Charles says was familiar to all the writers of the New Testament, is full of eschatological matter of a sort, but for our purpose it will suffice to examine one passage.[3] This passage is taken from an exceedingly old portion of the apocalypse, whose ulterior date is fixed at the year 170 B.C.[4] It deals, in contrast to much of the work, with the state of the *human* dead, and has the additional advantage of bearing the direct vision form.

Enoch sees deep, dark, "smooth" holes[5] in which the souls are confined until the Day of Judgment. "Sheol," then, is in this passage but another name for the intermediate state.[6] The division of Sheol, which is greatly elucidated by Dr. Charles' instructive notes, is fourfold. First, "And I saw the spirits of the children of men who were dead, and their voice penetrated to the heaven and complained." These are the souls of the righteous who have, for their righteousness' sake, suffered an unmerited death. Separated from these, and forming the second division, are the other souls of the righteous, and in their abode there

[1] *Encycl. Bibl.*, Art. "Apocal. Lit."
[2] *The Book of Enoch.*, ed. by R. H. Charles, D.D., Gen. Intr., p. 1.
[3] *Op. cit.*, p. 94.
[4] *Encycl. Bibl.*, Art. "Apocal. Lit.," iii.
[5] Dr. Charles, *loc. cit.*, understands this as referring only to the place of punishment.
[6] But see *op. cit.*, note on lxiii. 10.

is "a spring of the water of life." This will recall previous Hebrew Revelations, and that of St. John in the canon. This is not the only mention of the water of life in *Enoch*, and it should be connected, of course, with the old classical rivers of Hades. The third department of Sheol "has been made for sinners when they die and are buried in the earth without incurring judgment in their lifetime." "Here," continues Rufael, the angel guide, "their souls are placed apart in this great pain, till the great day of judgment and punishment and torture of the revilers for ever, and vengeance for their souls, there will they be bound for ever." One point in this is already familiar: from the very earliest times burial had an important influence on the state of the dead, a fact for which abundant evidence has already been adduced. Lastly, there is still another division of Sheol for the souls of those who "complain and make known their destruction when they were slain in the days of the sinners." The following verse explains this, and foretells the ultimate doom of the class. "Thus it has been made for the souls of men who were not righteous but sinners, complete in their crimes: they will be with criminals like themselves; but their souls will not be slain on the day of judgment, nor will they be raised from thence."

It is worth while to sum up the result of these quotations. The classification is briefly as follows:—First, the righteous unjustly done to death; second, other righteous souls; third, the wicked unpunished in this life (and peacefully buried); and fourth, the wicked who have on earth made partial atonement for their sins. The phrase applied to the third class, "their souls will not be slain in the day of judgment," demands an explanation. This slaying of the soul, as Dr. Charles points out, did not mean annihilation: it was the worst penalty Hell had to inflict, and as the better class of sinners are here exempted from it, it is, by a fair implication, the condemnation of the worst class, the prosperous sinners of the third division.

This very brief account should not be closed without some words as to the nature of the heaven and hell which Enoch presents. Anything very definite is unfortunately impossible, as, on the one hand, when he appears to be writing about heaven, Enoch is often only describing the Messianic kingdom; and, again, when he writes of hell, he is almost always depicting the place of punishment of the "stars" or fallen angels. Some conception, however, of both places it is legitimate to gather in this indirect way; and it is enough here to say that Enoch does not contain any surprises. The site of heaven and its imagery vary in the different sections of the work: and as for hell, Enoch does not go far beyond a chaos of fire, chains of iron, scourges, and such commonplaces of physical torture.

"In *The Slavonic Enoch*," says Dr. Charles,[1] "... we have, so far as I am aware, the most elaborate account of the seven heavens that exists in any

[1] *Book of the Secrets of Enoch*, Intr., p. xxxvi.

writing or in any language." Were the topography of the celestial spheres our immediate concern, a full account of the work would be instructive; but, considered ethically, these sevenfold schemes of heaven are almost invariably disappointing. The present system is certainly more interesting than its class, and contains, besides, even closer parallels to the later Christian vision-writers. A summary, which will be as brief as possible, must therefore be given.

First, then, it is noticed that the two angels who appear to conduct Enoch to heaven bear quite a striking resemblance to those of St. Peter's Apocalypse, which it would be a mistake, however, to press too far, as there is not an infinite possibility of variety in such a description.

Enoch travels on moving clouds through air and then through ether, and arrives at the first heaven. Here is a very great sea, and, suggesting previous accounts, "the treasuries of the snow and ice, . . . of the clouds, . . . and of the dew."

The second heaven contains "prisoners suspended, reserved for and awaiting the eternal judgment." The whole is in darkness. But, unfortunately, the prisoners are not the human dead, but the fallen angels again.

The description of the garden, which is the third heaven, has already occurred, at least in part, and is destined to become more familiar. "And I saw all the trees of beautiful colours and their fruits ripe and fragrant, . . . springing up with delightful fragrance." The tree of life "cannot be described for its excellence and sweet odour." From its roots flow the four rivers, first to the Paradise of Eden, "between corruptibility and incorruptibility," and afterwards to the earth. The third heaven is prepared as an eternal inheritance for the righteous, especially such as have been persecuted in their lives. In the "northern region," however, of this same heaven is situated the place of chastisement. It appears [1] that the idea of the wicked being punished in a division of heaven is not foreign to Hebrew thought, especially in its earlier stages; but this is the first mention in an apocalypse of such an apparent contradiction. One or two vague pagan systems, such as those of Er, Scipio, or Thespesius, seem to allow of a similar though much less definite interpretation, but the presence of anything wicked in heaven is of very infrequent occurrence. We are to see how a later vision explicitly interposes the firmament between heaven and all wickedness, and this represents the ordinary belief. Indeed, Enoch himself, in a later passage,[2] uses these words, which seem to imply the more usual topography, and therefore to be inconsistent with the present passage: "All things that exist I have written down, the height from earth to the seventh heaven, and down to the lowest hell, the place of judgment, and the mighty hell laid open, and full of lamentation." The scheme of punishment presents no remarkable features; the incidentals are already familiar—impenetrable gloom, a fiery river, and the alternation of flames and ice.

[1] Charles, *op. cit.*, x. 1, note. [2] Chap. xl. 12.

APOCRYPHAL LITERATURE

The catalogue of sinners contains one addition, which, with the partial exception of a few words in *The Revelation of Moses*, is new, but which will recur:[1] those "do not know their Creator, and have worshipped gods without life, who can neither see nor hear, being vain gods; and have fashioned the form of idols, and bow down to a contemptible thing made with hands."

The remaining heavens of this vision are irrelevant; in the seventh, hosts of angels make obeisance to the Lord, "in boundless light singing songs with low and gentle voices, and gloriously serving Him."

With only two further quotations, from the later part of the work,[2] this account may be closed. The first reverts to the description of hell, and emphasises the eternality of punishment. "I saw those who keep the keys and are the guardians of the gates of hell, standing, like great serpents, and their faces were like quenched lamps, and their eyes were fiery, and their teeth were sharp, and they were stripped to the waist. And I said before their faces, 'Would that I had not seen you, nor heard of your doings, and that those of my race had never come to you. Now they have only sinned a little in this life, and always suffer in the eternal life.'" Again, some verses concerning the joys of Paradise are pushed home and enforced by a series of beatitudes quite scriptural in tone, of which the first and most general may be given. It reads thus: "I tell you, my children: blessed is he who fears the name of the Lord, and serves

[1] See above, p. 110, and below, p. 131.   [2] Chap. xlii.

continually before His face, and brings his gifts with fear continually in this life, and lives all his life justly, and dies." This, too, is interesting, and seems to contradict a passage in *The Revelation of Moses:* "And now, my children, do not say, 'Our father stands before God, and prays for us to be released from sin'; for there is no person there to help any man who has sinned."

It would be possible to prolong this section by adducing evidence from several other apocalypses of neighbouring date, but it has already assumed considerable proportions, and it is doubtful if much would be added to the conception of the other world at which we have already arrived. *The Ascension of Isaiah*, for instance, includes another *locus classicus* for the sevenfold division of heaven, but it is quite without importance to the present subject, with the exception of one passage which has already been quoted in support of the " Descensus Christi." An imperfect scheme of seven heavens is found in a Greek *Apocalypse of Baruch*,[1] discovered only a few years ago in the British Museum. This work contains other points of interest. First, there is, apparently in the third heaven, a great dragon which eats the bodies of the wicked, and thrives on them. This recalls our earliest monster, that Ammet which devoured the sinners of the vision of Setme.[2] Also, it is interesting to find in Baruch's fifth heaven close

---

[1] Ed. by Dr. James, *Texts and Studies*, vol. v. No. 1.
[2] Above, pp. 21, 24.

resemblance with *The Apocalypse of Paul*, the same gates inscribed with the names of the just, and a similar system of guardian angels who bear the deeds of men to heaven.[1] Paul's Acherousian Lake[2] also is found in another Jewish vision, the Greek *Apocalypse of Moses:*[3] in the Hebrew work Adam is washed there and left for three hours, by one of the six-winged seraphim.

Finally, there are a few individual characteristics in a Coptic fragment edited and translated alongside of *The Apocalypse of Elias* by Steindorf.[4] This vision is either, as Steindorf thinks, anonymous, or should be connected, as others[5] take it, with the single page by Zephaniah, which is discussed in the same place. The narrator visits hell first, and then crosses in a boat to heaven, but the separation of the two is by no means complete, and the most striking details of chastisement are seen in the second part of the vision, when heaven opened itself from east to west and from north to south, thus giving a second view of the infernal torments, presumably beneath. The gates of hell are of brass, with brazen locks and iron keys, and shoot out flames about fifty "stadia" in length. Hell itself is a vast lake of sulphurous fire, like mud, in which the sinners are variously tormented, bound or blinded or scourged as their

---

[1] See below, pp. 141, 143.   [2] See below, p. 145.
[3] Tischendorf, *Apocal. Apocr.*
[4] Gebhardt und Harnack, *Texte und Untersuchungen*, Neue Folge II.
[5] *Encycl. Bibl.*, Art. "Apocrypha," § 21.

case may be. Some are wrapped in mats of fire, which is an Egyptian touch. The Old Testament patriarchs and saints intercede daily for these miserable wretches, whose penalties they are able in this vision to see; (this is further evidence of the imperfect division of heaven and hell). The various angels have rolls in which they enter the names and deeds of men, and the Book of Life occupies a prominent position. The description of the angels of punishment is not without merit. Their face was like a panther's, their teeth projected from their mouths like those of a bear, their eyes were bloodshot, and their hair streaming like a woman's, and they carried burning scourges in their hands. There is one further curious detail. The souls of sinners [1] are compelled to whirl about in the air for three days with the angels who fetch them at death, before they are carried off to everlasting torment. It is certainly strange to find so early one of Dante's most familiar conceptions, doubly immortalised by its connection with the pathetic story of Francesca da Polenta.

Christian Visions.

The Apocalypse of Peter.

It is hardly too much to say that *The Apocalypse of Peter* is the most important Christian vision that has survived from the first centuries of our era. How nearly it did not survive appears

[1] ἀσεβεῖς, Gottlosen.

from the fact that the MS. was only discovered in 1892. St. Peter's is the earliest of the Christian apocalypses, and its recovery supplies a link that has long been wanting in what may be called the apocalyptic chain which binds the period immediately before and after the birth of Christ to the Middle Ages. For if a thought be given to the details of the Hebrew visions which have been summarised above, there will surely be no two opinions as to what were at least some of the sources from which Peter drew. On the other hand, it would be hard to estimate the extent of the influence of this apocalypse: it can be traced directly in succeeding visions of the apocryphal period, and indirectly in many of the legends of the Middle Ages, and even in Dante himself. This being the case, Peter's apocalypse being as it were the Christian ancestor of the family of which a survey is now to be taken, it is necessary to give the particulars of it in detail. The MS., as recovered, is incomplete; nearly three-fourths of the fragment is transcribed here, from Dr. M. R. James' translation,[1] which appeared immediately after the text was first seen in Cambridge. Some further details, mostly of an unpleasant nature, can be gathered from half a dozen sentences quoted by writers of the early centuries of the Christian era, but, with one partial exception, not occurring in our present text.

The vision really begins in the third section of

[1] Camb. Univ. Press, 1892. Dr. James' verse numbers are retained for convenience of reference. His italics mark restorations of lacunæ.

the fragment, in Dr. James' edition. In the second section the apostles ask Christ to show them one of their "righteous brethren that had departed from the world"; their desire is gratified, and the third and part of the fourth paragraphs are taken up with a description of the two righteous souls whose beauty dazzles the eyes of the wondering twelve. From this point, in section 4, the remainder of the fragment is relevant and necessary, and is accordingly appended in full. The author, it should be noticed, continues in the first person singular; the previous vision has been granted also to his fellow-disciples.

"And I said to Him: 'And where are all the righteous, or of what sort is the world wherein they are and possess this glory?'

"5. And the Lord showed me a very great space outside this world shining excessively with light, and the air that was there illuminated with the rays of the sun, and the earth itself blooming with unfading flowers, and full of spices and fair-flowering plants, incorruptible and bearing a blessed fruit: and so strong was the perfume that it was borne even to us from thence. And the dwellers in that place were clad in the raiment of angels of light, and their raiment was like their land: and angels ran about (*or* encircled) them there. And the glory of the dwellers there was equal, and with one voice they praised the Lord God, rejoicing in that place. The Lord saith unto us: 'This is the place of your predecessors (*perhaps* brethren) the righteous men.'

"6. And I saw also another place over against that other, very squalid, and it was a place of chastisement; and those that were being chastised, and the angels that were chastising, had their raiment dark, according to the atmosphere of the place.

"7. And there were some there hanging by their tongues; and these were they that blaspheme the way of righteousness: and there was beneath them fire flaming and tormenting them.

"8. And there was a certain great lake full of flaming mire, wherein were certain men that pervert righteousness; and tormenting angels were set upon them.

"9. And there were also others, women, hung by their hair over that mire that bubbled up: and these were they that had adorned themselves for adultery: and the men that had been joined with them in the defilement of adultery *were hanging* by their feet, *and* had their heads in the mire: *and all* were saying, 'We believed not that we should come into this place.'

"10. And I saw the murderers and them that had conspired with them cast into a certain narrow place full of evil reptiles, and being smitten by those beasts, and wallowing there thus in that torment: and there were set upon them worms as it were clouds of darkness. And the souls of them that had been murdered were standing and looking upon the punishment of those murderers, and saying, 'O God, righteous is Thy judgment.'

"11. And hard by that place I saw another narrow place, wherein the gore and the filth of them that were tormented ran down, and became as it were a lake there. And there sat women having the gore up to their throats, and over against them a multitude of children *which* were born out of due time sat crying: and there proceeded from them *flames* (*or* sparks) of fire, and smote the women upon the eyes. And these were they that *destroyed their children* and caused abortion.

"12. And there were other *men* and women on fire up to their middle, and cast into a dark place and scourged by evil spirits, and having their entrails devoured by worms that rested not: and these were they that persecuted the righteous and delivered them up.

"13. And hard by them again were women and men gnawing their lips, and being tormented, and receiving red-hot iron upon their eyes: and these were they that had blasphemed and spoken evil of the way of righteousness.

"14. And over against these were again other men and women gnawing their tongues and having flaming fire in their mouths: and these were the false witnesses.

"15. And in a certain other place were pebbles sharper than swords or than any spit, red-hot, and women and men clad in filthy rags were rolling upon them in torment: and these were the wealthy that had trusted in their wealth, and had not had pity upon orphans and widows, but had neglected the commandment of God.

APOCRYPHAL LITERATURE

"16. And in another great lake full of pitch and blood and boiling mire stood men and women up to their knees: and these were they that lent money and demanded interest on interest.

"17. And there were other men and women being hurled down from a great cliff, and they reached the bottom and again were driven by those that were set upon them to climb up upon the cliff, and thence they were hurled down again, and they had no rest from this torment.

(These were guilty of lewdness.)

"18. And beside that cliff was a place full of much fire, and there stood men who had made for themselves images instead of God with their own hands.

"19. And beside them were other men and women, who had rods, smiting each other, and never resting from this manner of torment.

"20. And others again near them, women and men, were burning, and turning themselves and being roasted: and these were they that had forsaken the way of God."

The most profitable sort of detailed comment upon this remarkable fragment will be to trace its specific influence upon later works of the same class, but a general remark may now be permitted. Even if it were necessary to admit that Peter had deliberately and entirely copied from the sources indicated in the previous section of this chapter, it would still be possible to admire his apocalypse for its very impressive realism. No one can help being struck by the serious precision of the present scheme. A very definite crime is punished by an as definite chastisement, and the impression of reality is in cases heightened by the presence of the victim as an onlooker and approver of the doom. Monstrous and impossible angels and grotesque caricatures of fiends have, for the present at least, been left behind, and by his simple and direct treatment of borrowed detail Peter has produced an effect which the fantastic originals could never approach to achieving.

The History of Barlaam and Josaphat.

From this work, Dr. James [1] and Canon Robinson [2] both quote two visions in which they find evidence of a knowledge of *The Apocalypse of Peter*. And indeed the traces are plainly to be read. A literal translation of the passages [3] will now be given. In the way of comment, we would only call attention to the fragrant flowers, and to the conception of heaven as a shining city, an idea which is already familiar. Josaphat is the beholder of the vision in both cases.

" He sees himself seized by certain fearful men, and traversing regions which he has never seen, and in a very great plain waving with flowers

---

[1] *Op. cit.*, p. 58 *seq*. The indebtedness of this section to Dr. James' lecture is by no means covered by one reference.

[2] *The Passion of St. Perpetua* (Texts and Studies, vol. i. No. 2), p. 37 *seq*.

[3] Translated from Boissonade, *Anecdota Græca*, vol. iv. p. 280.

blooming, and of a most sweet odour; there he beholds plants of all sorts and colours blossoming with certain strange and wondrous fruits, both very pleasant to see and desirable to touch. And the leaves of the trees whisper shrill with a very gentle breeze, giving out a fragrance when they are moved both unceasing[1] and most pleasant. And there were thrones set up, made of purest gold and precious stones, emitting a brilliant radiance like the day, and couches adorned with different coverings that surpass description for their beauty.[2] And waters flowed by, most transparent, and gladdening the very eyes. And when those fearful men had led him through this wondrous and great plain, they brought him into a city that shone with unspeakable brightness, having its walls of transparent gold, and its battlements built of stones which no one has ever seen. O! who could tell of the beauty of that city and its brightness? A light from above piercing strongly with its rays filled all the streets thereof; and certain winged hosts, each being a light to itself, dwelt there, chanting a strain never heard by mortal ear. And he heard a voice saying, 'This is the abode of the just; this is the blessedness of them that were well pleasing to the Lord.'

"And from that place those most horrible men led him away, and said that they were leading him backward. But, quite enchained by the delight and gladness of that place, 'Do not rob me,' he

[1] ἀκόρεστον, that does not satiate.
[2] Cf. above, Hebrew Visions, p. 112.

said, 'do not rob me, I importune you, of this unspeakable joy; but grant to me, too, to dwell in one corner of this very great city.' But they said, 'It is impossible now for thee to be there. But with much labour and sweat thou wilt come here, if thou dost force thyself.' This they said; and when they had gone through the very great plain, they took him off into dark places and filled with all unpleasantness, containing pain in measure equal to the brightness he had seen. And the whole place was filled with affliction and confusion. There a furnace was kindled,[1] enflamed with fire; and there were creeping there a sort of worms, for chastisement. And there were avenging powers presiding over the furnace, and certain men pitifully burned by the fire. And a voice was heard saying, 'This is the place of the sinners: this is the punishment of them that stained themselves with base deeds.' After this they led him out thence who also had led him in."

It is unnecessary to point out in detail the indebtedness of this vision to the fifth section of Peter's Apocalypse, and to the earlier Hebrew descriptions of heaven. The few lines of hell contain only the most ordinary ideas.

Of the second vision [2] only a few lines are relevant, which read as follows:—

"And he sees those fearful men, whom he had seen before, coming to him and leading him away to that very great and wondrous plain, and taking

---

[1] Translating v. l., ἐξήπτετο.
[2] Boissonade, *op. cit.*, vol. iv. p. 360.

him into the glorious and exceeding bright city. And as he came to the gate there met him others splendidly arrayed in great light, having garlands in their hands which shone with unspeakable beauty, such as the eyes of men never beheld." The remainder of the vision contains an interview with the dead Barlaam.

These two short passages are, it must be admitted, slight, but they have the merit of being succinct and graphic, and they present a view of heaven and hell which, as far as it goes, is not without interest. But above all things they are a valuable testimony to the influence which *The Apocalypse of Peter* and the earlier visions exerted.

The Passion of Saint Perpetua.

It seems best to take next in order another work which, as implied by a previous reference,[1] is connected with *The Apocalypse of Peter*. Canon Robinson argues that the last-named work is the common source of both *Barlaam and Josaphat* and *The Passion of St. Perpetua*. In spite of its curious stiff style, the latter is a pathetic story, and, besides, it contains a certain amount of new and interesting detail.

Perpetua recounts no less than four visions which were granted to her. The first, given in answer to her express prayers, disclosed to her that she and her companions were to suffer martyrdom. She saw a very narrow golden ladder stretching to

[1] To Armitage Robinson's *Passio S. Perpetuæ*.

heaven, bristling on both sides with knives, and under it a huge dragon couched waiting. Saturus, a fellow-prisoner, ascending first, turned, and said, "Perpetua, I am waiting for you; but be careful that the dragon do not bite you." "In the name of the Lord Jesus Christ," she answered, "he shall not hurt me." The dragon then raised its head as if in fear of her, and Perpetua ascended, treading upon the monster's head instead of the first rung of the ladder. Arrived at the top, she beheld Christ, "a white-haired man sitting in the dress of a shepherd, of large stature, milking sheep." "Many thousands" stood around Him in white robes; Christ welcomed Perpetua, and gave her a morsel of cheese, which she ate, "and all who stood around said 'Amen.'"[1] By this token Perpetua was made aware that her death was not far distant.

The vision, which at first sight may appear irrelevant, has been quoted at some length because of two important ideas in it. The figure of Christ as a shepherd is familiar, but now makes its first appearance in these pages; and secondly, we shall again meet with the ladder of Perpetua's vision, though not as a passage from earth to heaven, but as a form of torment in hell itself.[2] To modern taste there is something a little grotesque in Perpetua's account of her welcome in heaven, but in the monster and the knives of the ladder she has achieved a striking image of the martyr's end.

[1] Dr. Wallis' translation (Ante-Nicene Christian Library, vol. xiii.).
[2] See below, Vision of Alberic.

Perpetua's second and third vision show her her dead brother Dinocrates. This child had died a very early and very piteous death—" his face being so eaten out with cancer that his death caused repugnance to all men." Perpetua has been thinking of him, and praying for him, and on the same night sees him endeavouring in vain to drink out of a basin the edge of which is higher than his head. A succeeding vision, a few nights later, shows the boy in a far happier plight. "I saw that that place which I had formerly observed to be in gloom was now bright; and Dinocrates, with a clean body well fed, was finding refreshment. And where there had been a wound, I saw a scar; and that pool which I had before seen, I saw now with its margin lowered even to the boy's navel. And one drew water from the pool incessantly, and upon its brink was a goblet filled with water; and Dinocrates drew near and began to drink from it, and the goblet did not fail, and when he was satisfied, he went away from the water to play joyously, after the manner of children, and I awoke."

From this Perpetua says that she understood "that he was translated from the place of punishment," from which her readers must understand that she believed in the efficacy of prayers for the dead. The pains of Tantalus are, of course, of very frequent recurrence. We should perhaps notice the suggestion of the survival, on the other side, of physical disease.

There follows a brief vision of Saturus, in which

he sees himself and his fellow-prisoners transported into the glory of God. They are "gone out of the flesh," and are borne aloft by four angels whose hands do not touch them. The description of heaven follows closely the account of "Peter" and the Hebrew visions: "a vast space which was like a pleasure-garden, having rose-trees and every kind of flower. And the height of the trees was after the measure of a cypress, and their leaves were falling[1] incessantly." The martyrs also come to a place "the walls of which were such as if they were built of light," and at the gates of this city they are arrayed in white robes. They then enter into the presence of God, who is pictured as like a man with snow-white hair but with a youthful countenance. Saturus and his companions were nourished during their sojourn in heaven by "an indescribable odour, which satisfied us."

The Acts of Thomas.

From one passage of this long and fantastic apocryphal writing [2] it is possible to glean something for our subject. A woman, whom St. Thomas has been the means of restoring to life, relates her vision of the punishments of hell. It should be noticed that she is herself a particular sort of sinner, and her vision is coloured according to her own crime. "A certain man," she said, "received me, hateful in appearance, all black, and his clothing

---

[1] Much better "were singing" (ca*n*ebant for ca*d*ebant).

[2] Ante-Nicene Christian Library, vol. xvi. (Walker's translation).

APOCRYPHAL LITERATURE

exceedingly filthy; and he led me away to a place where there were many chasms, and a great stench and most hateful odour were given forth thence; and he made me bend down into each chasm, and I saw in the chasm blazing fire; and wheels of fire ran there, and souls were hung upon those wheels, and were dashed against each other. And there was then crying and great lamentation, and there was none released. And that man said to me, 'These souls are of thine own nation, and for a certain number of days they have been given over to punishment and torture; and then others are brought in instead of them; and likewise also these are again succeeded by others.'"

So far it has seemed advisable to quote, in order to call attention again[1] to the notion of a respite in penal suffering. Why the idea is introduced here it is difficult to conjecture, as the vision is not conspicuously charitable in other parts. There is a curious parenthesis a few lines later where this passage is repeated: talking of the alternation of chastisement, the woman states that of the souls "there are some also quite used up." Whether they are restored before the day of judgment, and if so, how, we are not informed. The vision, on the whole, is a rather dead and artificial production, and its obligations to "Peter" are many and obvious. The same squalid bestial crimes are punished, and the very details of the mode of punishment are borrowed. Even the infants of section 11 of "Peter" reappear to witness against their unnatural mothers

[1] See above, pp. 108, 109.

—" placed here for a testimony against them." Fire, mud, worms, hangings by tongue, by hair, and by feet, all these are reproduced with little noteworthy change: thieves and greedy, uncharitable persons are appropriately suspended by the hands—their guilty members.

The woman's guide, the man "all black," refuses to give her up to the chastising demons, as he has no authority to do so, and she presently finds herself once more in the land of the living.

The Apocalyse of Paul.

The Apocalypse of Paul is altogether a bigger and more interesting work than the three which have just been noticed, and it will be necessary to give a somewhat full account of it. The influence of "Peter" and of various Hebrew visions can be traced in abundance here also, but it would be unfair to regard "Paul" as quite unoriginal. Coincidences have now become too numerous and too obvious to give to each a special acknowledgment.

Only at section 11 does the vision [1] begin to be relevant to our subject. It is therefore necessary to pass over the interesting passage which deals with the reports of all the deeds of men, conveyed every night and every morning to God by the guardian angels of the human race. This conception is already familiar, from the Greek "Baruch." In section 11, his angel guide undertakes to show

[1] Rutherford's trans. (Ante-Nicene Christ. Lib., Addit. vol., p. 152).

St. Paul "the place of the just," and the souls of sinners in the abyss. First he is conducted to heaven, and looking back, sees, under the firmament, "oblivion which deceives and draws to itself the hearts of men," and all the spirits of evil, and the princes of vices. There is a resemblance here to *The Ascension of Isaiah*, where all the powers of wickedness are also shut off from heaven by the firmament. Again looking back, St. Paul saw "angels without mercy . . . whose countenance was full of madness, and their teeth sticking out beyond the mouth . . . and from the hairs of their head sparks of fire went out, or from their mouth." These were the fiends "destined to the souls of the impious," and the apostle saw another group of angels "whose countenance shone as the sun, . . . having palms in their hands, and the sign of God," who were sent to lead the souls of the just to heaven.

The ensuing passage recalls a Latin pagan vision, of which an account has already been given. St. Paul is bidden to look down at the earth, and, doing so, he "wondered, and said to the angel, 'Is this the greatness of men?'"

St. Paul now looked down again to the earth, and saw a just man on the point of death, and all his works and all his desires, "both what he remembered, and what he did not remember," stood in his sight in his hour of need. Angels, both holy and impious, attended at his death-scene, "but the impious found no place of habitation in him, but the holy took possession of his soul, guiding it till it went out of the body." These same holy angels then received the soul at death with kisses and words of advice and encouragement, amongst other things bidding him remember his body, for he would have to return to it at the resurrection. The just soul's own guardian angel then leads it to heaven (ineffectually challenged on the way by an impious angel), and Michael and "all the army of angels" introduce it to the presence of its God, where it is welcomed by "a thousand thousand angels and archangels and cherubim, and twenty-four elders singing hymns and glorifying the Lord . . ." Such passages need no comment: they must have a familiar air to every one, and the set of ideas which is universally known through the canonical Apocalypse has been laid under obvious tribute.

At this point it is possible to abbreviate this abstract considerably, as St. Paul proceeds to relate the exactly opposite death-scene of a wicked man. It is only necessary, then, to imagine the whole process reversed. The wicked soul, too, is taken to God, but only to be condemned. The spirits of evil under the firmament challenge his approach, but he must be admitted for judgment. The angels in heaven cannot abide his presence, for "the stink of him crosses to us angels." His "spirit" that has lived in him from birth, joins his guardian angel in accusing him, and a voice is heard saying, " . . . Let him therefore be handed over to the angel Tartaruch, who is set over the punishments, . . . and let him be there

APOCRYPHAL LITERATURE

till the great day of judgment." Here there follows a clear reminiscence of " Peter," section 10 : " . . . I heard the voice of angels and archangels saying, 'Thou art just, Lord, and Thy judgment is just.'"

The next two sections of the work, the 17th and 18th, contain a more detailed judgment scene, in which a wicked soul is confronted with the souls of those whom he has wronged on earth. This wretched soul has lived unrepentant in wickedness to the day of his death. God's mercy is incidentally exhibited: "'For by Myself,'" He says, "'I swear, and by My holy angels, and by My virtue, that if he had repented five years before he died, on account of one year's life, oblivion would now be thrown over all the evils which he sinned before, and he would have indulgence and remission of sins.'" But now he is condemned till the day of judgment to the torments of hell's "lower prison"; and again the angels unite to praise the justice of God's judgments.

The angel now leads St. Paul to the third heaven, where there is a door of gold with two golden columns, on which are inscribed "the names of the just, serving God with their whole heart, who dwell on the earth." The apostle observes from this that the just are known in heaven even before their departure from this life. Entering into Paradise, (here in the third heaven, but not always thus), St. Paul meets and converses with Enoch and (probably) Elijah. The modesty of the apostle would not enjoy its present repute if his

Apocalypse were the only means of estimating it. His Christian work meets with the most liberal recognition from most of the saints with whom, both now and later in the work, he has speech.

Section 21 is important. Descending from the third heaven through the second, and on to the firmament, St. Paul comes out through the doors of heaven into the "land of promise." This is the land which is to be revealed at the Second Coming of Christ, when the first earth is dissolved, "and then the Lord Jesus Christ, the King Eternal, will be manifested, and will come with all His saints to dwell in it, and He will reign over them a thousand years . . ." Not only this, but in the meantime it is the "earth" which the "meek" of the Beatitudes inherit. Here the souls of the just abide till the day of judgment. The place is by the river Oceanus, and "the land there is seven times brighter than silver."

The special place in the land of promise set apart for the souls of the married, through which flowed the river of milk and honey, fringed by trees of marvellous growth, is an obvious absurdity. The well-known doctrine of St. Paul perhaps demanded recognition, but it cannot be said that the author of the Apocalyse has commended the theory by his treatment.

St. Paul is then conducted to "the Acherousian Lake where is the City of Christ." This city was built of gold, and surrounded by twelve walls, with twelve inner towers. In the walls were twelve gates, and round the whole flowed four rivers, bearing the names of the rivers of Eden. This is the Heavenly Jerusalem, the abode of all the righteous, (though two exceptional classes, the "meek" and the "married," have already been noted). Repentant sinners are only brought here by the angel Michael after being baptized in the Acherousian Lake. Outside the city gates, but not without hope of obtaining an ultimate entrance, are the souls of those who were zealous but proud.

St. Paul, drawing near to the city, meets at the first river, of honey, the prophets, who salute him; the souls of all who have denied themselves to do God's will are similarly brought, after death, to the prophets, who salute them as friends. At the river of milk the infants greet him, whom Herod slew: all pure persons after death are taken to receive the salutation of these infants. At the third river, of wine, on the north of the city, are other Old Testament saints: to them are brought the souls of such as received pilgrims. Near the fourth river, the river of oil, on the east, are the souls of those "who devoted themselves to God with their whole heart, and had no pride in themselves."

As the apostle proceeds, each of the twelve walls surpasses the last in size and glory. In each of the twelve gates sits a man on a golden throne, and there is a special "rank" of thrones, where those sit in unspeakable glory, who "made themselves fools for the sake of the Lord God." These were ignorant but very zealous, and in the presence of God the saints say of them, "Wait and see the unlearned who knew nothing more."

In the middle of the city is a high altar, and by it David leading the choirs of heaven: "there was one standing near the altar whose countenance shone as the sun, and he held in his hands a psaltery and harp, and he sang psalms, saying 'Halleluia.'" The whole city responds, and so it will be at the Second Coming of Christ. A curious section (30) follows, which obscurely explains the word "alleluia," and incidentally condemns the practice of not joining in responses at church.

Here the account of heaven ends, and the apostle passes to more sombre scenes. Many of the details of his heavenly system are familiar from the New Testament: there is nothing that calls for special remark; the general verdict will probably be that St. Paul's heaven is very much what might be expected.

The travellers now leave the city behind them, and cross the river of milk and honey, and the stream Oceanus, which surrounds the earth and on which the "beginning of heaven" is founded. "And when I was at the outer limit of Ocean, I looked, and there was no light in that place, but darkness and sorrow and sadness." First St. Paul came to a boiling river of fire, in which men and women were plunged up to several depths. The various depth of immersion must be taken to correspond with the writer's estimate of the crime, but the graduation does not appear to represent any

APOCRYPHAL LITERATURE

very deliberate ethical scheme. The souls in the river are the "neither hot nor cold," who have spent their lives in vacillation between righteousness and sin, and who, it will be remembered, were more leniently treated in a much earlier vision.[1] Those who wrangle after church are immersed up to the knees; burning to their middle are those who, "when they have taken the body and blood of Christ," relapse into sensual sin. "Detractors of each other when they assemble in the church of God" are buried in fire to the lips; "those up to the eyebrows are those who nod approval of themselves and plot spite against their neighbours." It is superfluous to mention Dante.

Next an abyss for "those who did not hope in the Lord," the depth of which the souls hardly plumb in fifty years. In this context it may be remarked that many of our visions are so prodigal of torments and places of torment that they become inconsistent and vague. Obviously the people of the fiery river might, many of them, if not all, have been consigned to this abyss. This feature of the literature of visions hardly constitutes a serious difficulty, but it must be borne in mind that when large classes are mentioned, there will always be exceptions to them. Besides, as we have already had occasion to observe, no classification can be satisfactory: what soul will only merit chastisement for one specific offence? This point is a subject of comment in editions of Dante.

[1] Setme, see above, pp. 22, 24.

St. Paul then turned his attention again to the fiery river, and beheld in succession a presbyter, a bishop, a deacon, and a reader undergoing special penalties in consideration of their office. It is not necessary to enter into further detail, but it is impossible to pass over the terribly appropriate and realistic fate of the last-named, "who read to the people, but he himself did not keep the precepts of God." This poor wretch was plunged to the knees in the river of fire, and "then came the angel who was set over the punishments, having a great fiery razor, and with it he cut the lips of that man and the tongue likewise." It is the main facts, however, that are important, for they point unmistakably to a considerable prevalence of misconduct amongst the officers of the Church of that day. When the writer of an apocalypse becomes specific, it is especially safe to infer that he is drawing upon his own experience, and has some definite object in view. The present passage, then, is best understood as a solemn warning to the ecclesiastical authorities of the period. This is not the earliest occurrence of such a passage, nor will it be the last.

Space forbids more than a mere catalogue of the ensuing punishments. The obligation of the list to *The Apocalypse of Peter* will not escape notice.[1] Usurers are consumed by worms. Inattention in church, which is disparagement of God's word, is punished in a fire where the guilty gnaw their own tongues. Dealers in the "black

[1] For details, see Trans. quoted.

APOCRYPHAL LITERATURE

art" are found in a pit immersed in fire (or blood[1]) up to the lips. Adulterers suffer in a pit of fire, with their faces black, and "girls having black raiment," with burning chains thrown round their necks, are those who had, unknown to their parents, sacrificed their honour. Persecutors of widows and orphans and of the poor are devoured by worms in a place of ice and snow, their hands cut and their feet naked. The pains of Tantalus are the doom of those who "broke their fast before the appointed hour," that is before the early sacramental service. Other carnal sinners were hanging by their eyebrows or hair in a fiery river, while the worst of all were covered with dust, with faces like blood, "in a pit of pitch and sulphur and running down into a fiery river." In a pit, also, in bright garments, but with their eyes blind, are those who gave alms, but not from the only proper motive: they "knew not the Lord God." The class of fleshly sinners dealt with in section 11 of Peter's Apocalypse[2] are here torn in pieces by wild beasts in a fire. Their infants are again represented as bearing witness against them, but in the present vision they have given their testimony at the trial of the soul, and have themselves been led by the angels of Tartarus into "a wide place of mercy." Last of this division of the punishments is the place allotted to those in whom the spirit of world-

---

[1] This interpretation is perhaps open to question. But the absence of any specific mention of fire, and the words, "his countenance was like blood," make it at least possible.

[2] See also Frag. 5 in Dr. James' edition.

liness was rampant, in spite of their seeming to "give up the world for God, putting on our garb . . ." Such were "clothed with rags full of pitch and fiery sulphur, and dragons were coiled about their necks and shoulders and feet, and angels having fiery horns restrained them, and smote them, and closed their nostrils."

This might appear to be enough of horror, but St. Paul is told to spare his lamentations; he is yet to see punishments "seven times greater than these." This must be admitted, however, to be quite a false alarm. The whole construction of this passage is a valuable index to the purpose of the work. The reader is led to expect great things, and is bound to regard what follows as the climax of sin and punishment, at least in the opinion of the author. What actually does follow is this: St. Paul saw a sort of well, sealed with seven seals, and when these were broken "there arose from it a certain hard and malign stench." Whoever had been thrust through the narrow mouth of this well, of him there was no more remembrance in heaven. "Who are these, sir," the apostle inquires, "who are put into this well?" "They are whoever shall not confess that Christ has come in the flesh and that the Virgin Mary brought Him forth, and whoever says that the bread and cup of the Eucharist of blessing are not this body and blood of Christ." Again, cold, snow, gnashing of teeth, and two-headed worms are the fate of those who deny the fact of Christ's resurrection and the certainty of their own. We have left morals, then, and arrived at the chastisement of heresies; we are at once in an ecclesiastical atmosphere of doctrine, and we feel the jealousy with which the author seeks to guard the dogmas of his Church.

Here the eschatological portion of the apocalypse may almost be said to come to an end, and the remainder may therefore be very briefly summed up in conclusion. In answer to St. Paul's prayers for mercy on behalf of the souls in hell, he sees the heaven move like a tree and the Son of God Himself descends and grants them a weekly respite from their torment. "On the day on which I rose from the dead I gave to you all who are in punishment a night and a day of refreshment for ever." This Christ is represented as doing, amongst other reasons, "because of Paul, the well-beloved, whom I would not vex." With the facts of the intermission of torment we are already familiar, but this naïve explanation of them is new and unique.

The apostle now returns to Paradise, whither it is scarcely necessary to accompany him. He sees the trees of Eden, the Tree of Life and of the Knowledge of Good and Evil. He meets and talks with the Virgin Mary, and with numerous patriarchs, saints, and prophets, with some of whom he has already conversed earlier in the account. The MS., from the translation of which we have quoted, breaks off very abruptly, but the translator quotes a version of a Syriac MS. which gives the natural conclusion to the vision, beginning, "And the angel who was with me led me forth . . ."

Minor Visions.

The foregoing apocalypse is so complete, that, taken in conjunction with "Peter," it may be said to furnish an adequate conception of the heaven and hell of Christian apocryphal literature. It remains, however, to notice some details peculiar to further visions of the same class, avoiding pointless repetition as much as may be.

First, then, are features of very special interest in *The Testament of Abraham*,[1] which vividly recall one of the earliest visions [2] recorded in these pages. The work seems certainly to have been composed by a Christian in Egypt. The details will speak for themselves. Abraham is led by the archangel Michael to the first gate of heaven, and sees there the broad and narrow ways of the New Testament,[3] the one conducting the just through a narrow gate to life, and the other thronged by seven times as many souls, leading the wicked through a broad gate to destruction. Adam sat on a glorious throne between the gates, and mourned or rejoiced according to the direction taken by the majority, but "his weeping exceeded his laughing sevenfold." It is inside these gates that the very striking Egyptian detail occurs. Here, on a terrible throne between the gates, is

---

[1] Ante-Nicene Christ. Lib., Addit. vol., p. 183 *seq*. Intr. and trans.
[2] Setme, above, p. 19 *seq*.
[3] And, we may add, of the poet Hesiod, (Works and Days, 286 *seq*.).

Abel, the son of the first man, judging all mankind. Before his throne is a table, "like crystal, all of gold and fine linen," and on it a book, "the thickness of it six cubits, and the breadth of it ten cubits." To right and left stand recording angels, who enter in the book, each on his own side, the good and bad deeds of the soul at the bar. In front of the table sits an angel, Dokiel, holding a balance, and on his left Puruel, an angel "all fiery, pitiless, and severe," who tests by fire the deeds of men. If the fire refuses to consume a man's works, "the angel of righteousness takes him and carries him up to be saved in the lot of the just." The parallel, even so far, would be sufficiently complete, but it is enormously strengthened by what follows. One soul is presently "set in the midst," neither dismissed to hell nor carried up to heaven, and the explanation of Michael runs thus: "Because the judge found its sins and its righteousness equal, he neither committed it to judgment nor to be saved, until the Judge of all shall come." (Abraham and the archangel intercede for this soul, and when Abraham looks up after praying it is gone to Paradise.)

The Testament of Abraham must not be left without a word upon the really fine picture of the Angel of Death which fills the last five chapters of the work. Death comes to Abraham like an archangel, glorious and bright and beautiful, and so, he says, he appears to all the just. At the patriarch's request, however, he assumes in turn the terrific forms in which the wicked behold him, and awful indeed is the change. The passage is very well worth reading.

The Apocalypse of Esdras[1] is obviously indebted to both "Peter" and "Paul," and contains absolutely nothing which seems to demand quotation here. The same remark and the same references will cover *The Apocalypse of John*, which is largely prophetic of the Second Coming of Christ, and draws extensively upon the New Testament, and especially upon the imagery of the "Revelation" there. The curious *Narrative of Zosimus*[2] describes the state of the blessed, but they are not in heaven; indeed, they have been brought in the body to the place they inhabit, and are after many years subject to a death of a mild form, after which they are taken by angels to worship God in "the firmaments." The means by which Zosimus obtained his vision of these holy men recall details which are already familiar.[3] After he has prayed and fasted, a camel conveys him to the bank of an impassable river in the desert. Here he again resorts to prayer, and two fragrant trees spring up before his eyes, one on either side of the water. The tree on the hither side bends down, lifts the hermit and hands him over to the farther tree, which in turn stoops and deposits him in safety. And then we read, " And that place was filled with

---

[1] Tischendorf, *Apocal. Apocr.*, p. 24. Translated in Ante-Nicene Christ. Lib., vol. xvi. p. 468.

[2] Ante-Nicene Christ. Lib., Addit. vol., p. 219.

[3] See Dr. James' *Apoc. of Peter*, pp. 69, 70.

much fragrance, and there was no mountain on either hand, but the place was level and flowery, all crowned with garlands, and all the land beautiful."

Finally, mention should perhaps be made of a most glaring piece of plagiarism, *The Apocalypse of the Virgin*,[1] which is ascribed to as late a date as the ninth century. The author of this vision is not content with borrowing details of chastisement: he goes the length of picturing Christ as granting a respite on the Day of Pentecost to the damned, for the sake of His Virgin Mother's prayers. The belief in effectual intercession for the dead is common in Christian apocryphal visions, but it is not much strengthened by this feeble piece of imitation. It is to be feared that this apocalypse will be found more amusing than instructive. It has nothing significant to add to the descriptions of "Peter" and "Paul," and some of its variants from those systems of punishment are nothing short of ludicrous. Two instances must be allowed. "They who do not rise up to the presbyter when they enter into the church of God" are condemned to sit till the last judgment upon benches of fire; and an extraordinarily severe penalty is exacted from the widows of presbyters who had ventured to remarry after the death of their husbands: "And she saw women hanging by their nails, and a flame of fire came out of their mouth and burned them: and all the beasts coming out of the fire gnawed them to pieces . . ." It is such passages as these

[1] *Texts and Studies*, ii. 3. Translated in Ante-Nicene Christ. Lib., Addit. vol., p. 169.

that throw a strange light upon the ages in which they passed as sacred and elevating literature. We have a protest, however, from a much more ancient period: "'The prophet that hath a dream, let him tell a dream; and he that hath My word, let him speak My word faithfully. What is the Chaff to the Wheat?' saith the Lord."

CHAPTER V.

EARLY CHRISTIAN LEGENDS.

IT is now necessary to hark back as far as the beginning of the Christian era, and in a sense to pick up the thread of the pagan visions for the second time. The first legend which is now to be mentioned is coupled with the name of a bishop of apostolic times. It will not be found, however, that we are in any way confused by this chronology. *The Apocalypse of the Virgin*, the latest of the writings above cited, in its matter and substance might well be contemporary with the works which will presently be quoted, and is in fact much more primitive in thought than some of these.

There is, however, one difference which makes itself felt almost from the first. The last chapter has been silent about one point which had figured in previous sections and is now to reappear. As early as the third century mention is made of Purgatory, and the conception lasts with no important break right up to the time of Dante, (and of course, further). Why does the idea take no place in the apocryphal literature? There the soul is represented as being judged at death and sent to torment or to bliss to await a second and final judgment. It has been shown how closely the apocryphal writers followed and copied a small number of originals, and it appears that the very definiteness of those upon the subject of the intermediate state has preserved the integrity of their doctrine. But assuming an intermediate state, the notion of Purgatory was inevitable. There have always been minds to rebel against the eternality of future chastisement, and to welcome a belief which held out a prospect of further progress and of nobler character. How dangerous the doctrine has been, and how terribly abused, a study of its vision literature is not the worst nor the least interesting method of discovering.

It should further be noted at this point, that henceforward it is only possible to tread in the footsteps of several exhaustive and learned authorities, some of whom have already been slightly quoted. Thomas Wright, in his *St. Patrick's Purgatory*, collected and arranged the mediæval legends in a way that elicited the highest praise from at least one eminent continental scholar. Another invaluable work is J. O. Delepierre's *L'Enfer, decrit par ceux qui l'ont vû*. Both books are now out of print; the latter can be seen in almost identical form in the Philobiblon Society's series (vols. viii. and ix.). Further, covering the same ground are A. F. Ozanam's *Des Sources Poétiques de la Divine Comédie* (*op. omn.*, vol. v. p. 397), and, not least helpful, an article entitled "La Divine Comédie avant Dante," by Charles Labitte. This last is perhaps most accessible in the *Revue des deux Mondes* (tome xxxi., quatrième serie). It is difficult indeed to follow where such scholars have led, but, even where the ground covered is the same, it is hoped that an arrangement, from a different point of view, of some of their copious material, may not be wholly unprofitable.

Saint Carpus.

The vision of Carp has other claims than its great age. It belongs to the class of visions which teach a specific lesson, here the lesson of charitableness. Examples of this order of legends have already been cited, and they become increasingly common in the Christian era. Carp is supposed[1] to be the bishop of Crete at whose house St. Paul, in his Second Epistle to Timothy,[2] says that he left a cloak. A letter of Dionysius the Areopagite[3] contains a full account of the vision. The bishop was much concerned at the time about the apostasy of a young and recent convert from the Greek Church. Awaking one night, as his habit was, to sing hymns, he prayed that both the young man and his friend who had led him astray might be consumed by fire, complaining "that it was not just that impious men should live and overset the right ways of the Lord." Thereupon his house was shaken and cleft from top to bottom, and a furnace appeared to him coming down from heaven.

---

[1] *Dict. Christ. Biog.*, sub voc.
[2] 2 Tim. iv. 13.
[3] Ep. viii. chap. 6. The Latin version has been followed.

Heaven itself, too, was opened, and on a ridge Carp saw Jesus surrounded by innumerable angels of human form. He then bent down and saw the earth split into a dark and gloomy chasm, on the brink of which, miserable and trembling, and "only not slipping in," stood the two youths who had been the subject of his prayer. Serpents from the gulf crept and wound about their feet, and men amongst the serpents struck and beat them. The bishop was pleased at their chastisement, richly deserved as he thought, and for some time kept his eyes fixed downwards on this scene. When he did again raise his eyes, he could hardly see heaven, but he saw enough to rebuke his vindictive severity. Jesus Himself rose from His throne, and, descending, stretched out His hand and took the young men out of the chasm. "Strike Me," He said to Carp, "as thy hand is already stretched out (to strike). For I am ready to suffer again for the salvation of men. And this is more pleasing to Me than that other men should sin. But see if it is well for thee to take thy dwelling[1] in the gulf and with the serpents rather than with God and His good angels who love mankind."

The Christian charity of this vision forms a contrast as striking as it is pleasing to the uniform severity of the literature which constituted the subject of the preceding chapter. Labitte,[2] apparently unfamiliar with the apocryphal visions, remarks of the leading features of the present story, "Voilà bien les merveilles des premiers temps du Christianisme." Certainly, but it is rather the

[1] *i.e.* fix thy thoughts. [2] *Op. cit.*, p. 712.

exceptional tone of this and one or two other stories that make us marvel, and not the general character of the early Christian apocalypse. It must be confessed that the vision has no direct bearing upon the state of the dead.

Three Monks and St. Macarius.

The Bollandists[1] are very suspicious as to this life of St. Macarius the Roman,[2] and reveal their attitude to the story and its otherwise unknown authors, the three monks, by printing it only in an appendix (to the 23rd of October) under the title, " De Fabuloso S. Macario Romano, etc." It appears that if the saint ever had any existence at all, it was about the end of the fourth century that he flourished: " S. Macarius autem in vivis repertus dicitur post Juliani Apostatæ cædem, anno Christi 363 peractam. . . ." Surius gives the story, under the same date, in his *De Probatis SS. Vitis.*[3]

Three monks of a monastery in Mesopotamia, named respectively Theophilus, Sergius, and Hyginus, determine to set out and find the place where heaven and earth join. It is impossible to linger over the details of their journey, though these are not without a certain interest, and we must be content with what concerns our subject. After a considerable period of wandering, then, the monks come to a place whence there smites them an in-

---

[1] *Acta Sanctorum*, Octobris, tom. x. p. 563.
[2] Labitte, *op. cit.*, p. 715; Wright, *op. cit.*, p. 95.
[3] Tom. iv. of the four volume edition, 1617-18.

tolerable stench, so that they fall fainting to the ground. Rising after a while, they behold a great lake full of blazing serpents, and hear voices of wailing and lamentation coming from it, saying: "Locus iste judicii et pænarum est, in quo cruciantur qui Christum negaverunt."

Further on the monks see a man of great stature—"quasi centum cubitorum," chained to two mountains, with a fire raging around him. Who this sufferer is, or what his crime, they do not hear, nor do they suggest to their reader. Again a little further, amidst great crags and in a deep place, they see a woman wound round and round by a terrible dragon, and as often as she opens her mouth to speak, the dragon thrusts in its head and bites her tongue. A little later there is a sentence which may account for the monks' silence as to these and other mysteries: "Venit ergo vox dicens: non est vestrum nosse mysteria, quæ vidistis: viam pergite vestram."

There can be no purpose served by entering into the description of the marvellous church of crystal where the monks presently find "holy men and honourable" singing praises. The passage abounds in the terms with which these pages are already familiar; but this is certainly no part of heaven, though it appears to be more than an ordinary church, and it must therefore be omitted now, with many other miracles incident to the journey.

Finally, then, the monks arrive at a cave, and after resting in it for a time, they come out and see a figure hastening towards them, whose hair, as white as milk or snow, covers his whole body. This is St. Macarius, and when the monks have removed his alarm, there follow many questionings on both sides. The saint informs the monks that they are only twenty miles from that paradise " ubi Adam et Eva in deliciis erant." He deprives them in the same breath of their hope of reaching it, however; for a cherubim with a whirling spear of flame stands before paradise to guard the tree of life; from foot to navel he is like a man, his breast is the breast of a lion, and he holds a sword in a hand of crystal, to ward off any who would approach.

The remainder of the story—St. Macarius' narrative of his wanderings and perils, and the marvels he has seen and done—is irrelevant, and it is to be feared that the information as to a future state which Macarius supplies is extremely scanty. But in justice to the three monks, it must be remembered that these topics are merely incidental to their life of St. Macarius, and are not the main subject of their writing.

St. Brandan.

The legend of the Voyage of St. Brandan,[1] the "Monastic Odyssey" as it has been called, is not very pregnant with eschatological meaning, but it is too curious and interesting to be left out of all account. The French scholar, M. Jubinal,[2] has

[1] Wright, *op. cit.*, p. 91.
[2] *La Légende Latine de S. Brandaines, avec une Traduction inédite en Prose et en Poésie Romanes*, Paris, 1836.

published a Latin text from MSS. which he assigns to the eleventh, twelfth, and thirteenth centuries, and the story is also accessible in the various editions and translations of the " Golden Legend." Mr. A. Nutt has made it the starting-point of his learned book, *The Voyage of Bran*, in the first part of which he reviews a very large number of legendary visits to the other world, including many of those which are here mentioned. St. Brandan was born about the year 482 or 484 A.D., and his voyage is assigned to the year 545.[1]

Instigated by the experience of a brother-abbot, Berinus by name, St. Brandan (whose name is subject to a variety of spellings), after due preparations and solemnities, set sail, with a company of fourteen monks and a crew, towards the East. It is not proposed to follow him in any detail. Suffice it to say that the saint's seven years' voyage consists of a more or less regular series of visits to certain marvellous islands, varied by perils of the deep in the intervals between. These islands are the Island of Sheep, where St. Brandan spends the days between Palm Sunday and Easter Eve; the Island of Birds, where he regularly spends his Eastertide; and the Island of the abbey, full of miracles, where the saint always keeps Christmas with the abbot and the four-and-twenty silent monks. The birds, by the way, are angels who fell with Lucifer, but their fault was very slight, and they are therefore free from all pain. Besides these three regular stopping-places, there may

[1] See *Dict. Christ. Biog.*, *sub voc.*, and references there.

EARLY CHRISTIAN LEGENDS

be mentioned the "quasi-island," so to speak, of the fish's back, on which the monks, at their first landing, light a fire, to the great inconvenience of the monster. "When the fire was right hot and the meat nigh sodden, then this island began to move, whereof the monks were afraid and fled anon to the ship and left the fire and meat behind them. And Saint Brandon comforted them, and said that it was a great fish named Jasconius, which laboured day and night to put his tail in his mouth, but for greatness he may not."[1]

There is no moral significance in all this, obviously, and it would be equally arbitrary to attach any such meaning to the incidents of the battle of the two great fishes, or the rout of the gryphon which attacks the monks' ship. Similarly the reader may make what he chooses of the audience of little fishes which crowd to the surface to hear the monks singing mass on St. Peter's Day.

There remain, then, the two or three paragraphs of the story which ought to be of some use to the present inquiry, but it must be confessed that with one important exception they are, eschatologically, barren. There is not much to be gleaned from a dark and smoky island full of stench and of the noise of bellows and of thunder, or, as Jubinal's text[2] has it, "sonitum follium sufflancium

---

[1] This and other English quotations are from *Leaves from the Golden Legend*, chosen by H. D. Madge, LL.M. (Constable, 1898).
[2] P. 40.

quasi tonitrua, atque malleorum collisiones contra ferrum et incudes." The demons who inhabit the island hurl lumps of molten metal from their forges at the ship, and even run along the top of the water in pursuit. This island is in the north, and presently, still farther in the same direction, a great mountain is reached, "all on fire and a foul smoke and stench coming from thence." Here St. Brandan loses one of his monks, who leaps into the sea and is carried off to hell by a crowd of demons.

Now follows what is by far the most impressive part of Brandan's story, so much so that the wisest course seems to be to quote the passage *in extenso*, and let it speak for itself. "And they came to a great rock standing in the sea: and thereon sat a naked man in full great misery and pain, for the waves of the sea had so beaten his body that all the flesh was gone off and nothing left but sinews and bare bones. And when the waves were gone, there was a canvas that hung over his head which beat his body full sore with the blowing of the wind. And also there were two ox-tongues and a great stone that he sat on which did him full great ease.

"And then Saint Brandon charged him to tell him what he was. And he said, 'My name is Judas, that sold Our Lord Jesus Christ for thirty pence, which sitteth here much wretchedly, howbeit I am worthy to be in the greatest pain that is. But Our Lord is so merciful that He hath rewarded me better than I have deserved; for of right my place is in the burning hell.[1] But I am here but certain times of the year, that is, from Christmas till the twelfth day, and from Easter till Whitsuntide be past, and every feastful day of Our Lady, and every Saturday noon till on Sunday the evensong be done. But all other times I lie still in hell in full burning fire with Pilate, Herod, and Caiaphas; therefore accursed be the time that I ever knew them.'

"And then Judas prayed Saint Brandon to abide still there all that night, and that he would keep him there still that the fiends should not fetch him to hell. And Saint Brandon said, 'With God's help thou shalt abide here all this night.' And then he asked Judas what cloth that was that hung over his head. And he said that it was a cloth that he gave to a leper, which was bought with the money that he stole from Our Lord when he bare His purse. 'Wherefore it doth to me full great pain now in beating my face with the blowing of the wind. And these two ox-tongues that hang here above me I gave sometime to two priests to pray for me. Them I bought with mine own money, and therefore they ease me, because the fishes of the sea gnaw on them and spare me. And this stone that I sit on lay sometime in a desolate place where it eased no man. And I took it thence, and laid it in a foul way, where it did much ease to them that went by that way.

---

[1] Judas is in as it were an isolated bit of hell. See Wright, *op. cit.*, p. 97, and the remarkable story there of the soul imprisoned in a block of ice taken by some fishermen in their net.

And therefore it easeth me now: for every good deed shall be rewarded, and every evil deed shall be punished.'

"And then Sunday against even, there came a great multitude of fiends blasting and roaring. And they bade Saint Brandon go thence that they might have their servant Judas: 'For we dare not come in the presence of our master, but if we bring him to hell with us.' And then said Saint Brandon, 'I hinder you not to do your master's commandment, but by the power of the Lord Jesus Christ, I charge you to leave him this night till to-morrow.' Thereto answered the fiends: 'How darest thou help him that so sold his master for thirty pence, and caused Him also to die the most shameful death upon the cross?' And then Saint Brandon charged the fiends by His Passion that they should not annoy him that night. And then the fiends went their way, roaring and crying, toward hell to their master the Great Devil. And then Judas thanked Saint Brandon so ruthfully that it was pity to see. And, on the morrow, the fiends came with an horrible noise, saying that they had that night suffered great pain because they brought not Judas: and said that he should suffer double pain the six days following. And they took then Judas, trembling for fear, with them to pain."

As a sample of the flavour of the Latin text, it may be permissible to quote a sentence or two which follows upon the return of the demons. "Demones dixerunt: 'Duplices sustinebit penas in istis diebus sex infelix iste Judas, pro eo quod illum defendistis in hac nocte.' Quibus Sanctus ait: 'Non habetis vos, inquit, potestatem ullam, neque princeps vester, quia potestas Dei erit.' Dixitque: 'Precipio vobis, inquit, in nomine Domini, et principi vestro, ne istum extollatis amplius cruciatibus, quam antea facere consuevistis.' Cui responderunt: 'Numquid tu dominus es omnium, ut tuis sermonibus obediamus?' Quibus vir Dei: 'Servus sum, inquit, Domini omnium, et quicquid in nomine ipsius precipio, fit; et non habeo ministerium nisi de his quos michi concedit.' Et ita eum sunt secuti blasphemiis insectantes, donec avelleretur a Juda. Demones autem reversi levaverunt infelicissimam animam inter se cum magno impetu et ululatu."

The excuse for the length of these citations must be the obvious literary merit of the descriptions and the real ethical import of the details of Judas' doom. It would be superfluous to go over these again, as they are quite plain to see, but special attention should be directed to the traitor's words regarding the stone upon which he sits. There is a world of significance in his three short sentences.

St. Paul the hermit, the quondam guardian of St. Patrick's Purgatory in Ireland, and his story of his miraculous life on the island where Brandan finds him, have no immediate bearing upon our subject, so we may accompany the saint at once to the Land of Promise towards which his whole voyage has been tending. It must be admitted at once that the end of the story is a terrible anticlimax. Nothing could possibly be more tame or uninteresting than the land which it has taken Brandan and his companions seven years of peril and hardship to find. It is a land full of trees and flowers and of equable temperature. There is a river there which the saint is not allowed to cross, and a "fair young man" who bids the band return for the present to their earthly abode, taking with them what they can carry of the fruits of this terrestrial Paradise. A poor meaningless piece of bathos, after the dangers which have been overcome to reach it. Our literature is full of disappointments of this sort, examples of such futile inconsequence of composition, that one is led to wonder how such stuff could be tolerated for a moment, much less revered and read with bated breath as something only second to the inspired writings of the Canon.

CHAPTER VI.

MEDIÆVAL LEGENDS.

THERE is not much to add, by way of introduction, to what has already been said at the beginning of the previous chapter. No new division of our subject is started at this point; the literature is practically uninterrupted, and the separation is chiefly a matter of chronology. It will be observed very soon, however, that the visions of the unseen are becoming more conscious, and therefore more elaborate. There is a growing tendency to use the vision form to enforce a homily, to impose a doctrine upon a superstitious people, to condemn, perhaps, an ecclesiastical irregularity, or even merely as an outlet for the superfluous literary energy of the monks. " Aussi chaque monastère avait son Recueil," says Delepierre,[1] "abrégé ou grossi selon le loisir de ses copistes." And there is abundant evidence that they did not strictly confine themselves to copying. The number of the visions becomes almost bewildering. The writer just quoted mentions in his bibliographical notes a work by a countryman of his own which

[1] *Op. cit.*, p. 31. He mentions the "Golden Legend" as the most famous.

refers the inquiring reader to no less than four hundred different authors who have written on the subject of a future state; and of these the number who do not adduce the testimony of visions must obviously be small. This curious and very learned book, *Recueil de Dissertations sur les Apparitions, les Visions et les Songes*, by Lenglet Dufresnoy, published in four duodecimo volumes, at Avignon, in 1751, is packed tight with stories of the supernatural, and includes many of the visions which are recorded in these pages.

Another strange work in two little volumes (which will be found interesting to the bibliophile, if not to the student) is Augustin Calmet's *Traité sur les Apparitions des Esprits et sur les Vampires, ou les Revenans*, etc. etc. (Paris, 1751). Older works of rather the same sort are the collection of Audradus Modicus and the famous *Dialogues* of Cæsarius of Heisterbach.

There are certain landmarks in the course which it is proposed to pursue through the mazes of this extensive literature, certain visions which stand out as being typical of the thought of their age. They are more elaborate than their contemporaries, and present really substantial conceptions and comprehensible doctrines. Such are the visions of St. Furseus, of Drihthelm, and Alberic, and particularly those of Tundal, Owain Miles, and Thurcill.

One other feature of the period may be simply mentioned at this point. A conception of hell will come under discussion which has only now in quite modern times won for itself a large acceptance. This might be called the spiritual conception in contrast to the entirely physical ideas of punishment which have hitherto prevailed. The notion is older than the Middle Ages, as will be shown in the proper place; but its appearance in the literature of visions is very late and very rare. The reason of this is obviously not far to seek. The spiritual conception does not lend itself readily to the apocalyptic form: it encourages no elaborate invention of detail, and is altogether less popular.

The Soldier of Gregory the Great.

There are some curious little glimpses of the unseen in the *Dialogues* of Gregory the Great,[1] who died in the year 604. While none of them are at all elaborate, their authorship must indubitably have tended to popularise this form of writing, and, what is more important, must have exercised a strong formative influence upon the mediæval doctrine of Purgatory.[2]

First, a monk named Peter, who had fallen sick and died, comes back to life, and relates that he has seen the "torments and innumerable places of hell." He himself was only rescued by an angel, who bade him return and look to himself how he led his life.

Next, a certain Stephen of Constantinople arrives before the judge of the dead. "I commanded not

[1] Bk. iv. chap. 36 *seq*. Trans. by Henry James Coleridge (London, 1874).
[2] *Dict. Christ. Biog.*, *sub voc*.

this man to be brought," says the latter, " but Stephen the smith." The wrong Stephen returns to life, and the decease of his unfortunate namesake verifies the vision.

The ensuing vision is the most important of the group, and contains one feature at least which is already prominent in the evolution of our subject. The soldier to whom the vision is ascribed saw a bridge stretching over a black smoky river, from which rose up a visible vapour of filthy smell. On the far side of the river men in white garments walked in pleasant meadows filled with flowers and with a fragrant odour. There were mansions in the meadows, and especially one built of gold bricks. Of the houses on the bank of the river, some were affected by the stench and others were not. The details of this scene will recall previous visions which we need not pause to name. The soldier further observed that while the good souls successfully negotiated the bridge, the bad fell off it into the river. This bridge will be found to recur in later visions, and meanwhile it need only be said that Labitte [1] describes it as a Persian idea, which has already passed into the Koran.[2]

The soldier then passes to particular cases of chastisement. He saw Peter, the steward of the Pope's household, who had been a cruel man, in a filthy place, bound and kept down by a weight. Is this a gentle warning to his successor in Gregory's establishment? Further, a certain Stephen was

[1] *Op. cit.*, p. 714. See Ozanam, *op. cit.*, p. 424 n.
[2] Cf. Addison's "Vision of Mirza" (*Spectator*).

observed to slip and half fall from the bridge, at which horrible men appeared endeavouring to drag him down into the filthy stream, while beautiful men resisted their efforts. The soldier awoke before he had time to see the issue of the struggle, but the interpretation of the incident is significant. The "horrible men" are the sins of the flesh, while their opponents are not the contrary graces of purity and abstinence, but the genii of a much more practical virtue, that of almsgiving!

Another vision follows, which resumes, in a way, the narrative of the soldier, and explains one of its figures. Old men and young men, girls and boys, were seen carrying bricks for the building of the houses of the soldier's vision. These houses, then, we must understand to be the heavenly counterparts and images of human lives, growing as they grow, and ready to receive the soul at death. By their houses ye shall know them! Every good deed is an added brick. The case of one "Deusdedit," a shoemaker, is instanced. This worthy man was accustomed to give away all his spare money in charity every Saturday at St. Peter's. On Saturdays, therefore, his heavenly mansion is abuilding. This is one of those visions which are almost worthless eschatologically, but invaluable as signs of the times.

The visions of the unruly boy Theodorus and of a Galatian monk, each in the grip of a dragon, are quite irrelevant. The chapter which follows these stories relates how a deacon named Paschasius was released from the pains of Purgatory by the prayers of Germanus, the bishop of Capua. The deacon had supported Laurentius in his candidature for the pontificate, and when his rival Symmachus was elected, did not transfer his allegiance. For this disloyal loyalty he was condemned to a rather amusing purgatory: he had to stand in the hot water, apparently, at a public bath, and it was there that Germanus had a vision of him, and was enabled, by his prayers, to obtain his release. The facts are trivial, but the main idea was worth noticing. Already it is believed that a soul may be released from the pains of Purgatory in answer to the prayers of a good churchman.

The theory that now and again a pagan could be rescued from everlasting damnation was an innovation upon the dogma of the early Church, and it appears that there is some reason for attributing it to Gregory the Great.[1] The Pope had conceived a great admiration for the Emperor Trajan, and devoted himself to prayer for the latter's soul. He was successful, and it is interesting that Dante[2] himself adopted a similar view of the Emperor's ultimate fate. Labitte remarks upon this as a rare clemency in the poet: "C'est la seule fois peut-être où le poète, égaré par le théologien, se soit departi de sa rigueur orthodoxe." Dante, it may be observed, declines the responsibility of placing either Trajan or Rhipeus the Trojan in the eagle's eyebrow as pagans; he is careful to explain that both have inherited the

[1] Labitte, *op. cit.*, p. 714.
[2] *Paradiso*, xx. 43 *seq.* (Plumptre).

joys of Paradise as Christians, but his readers are entitled to an opinion as to the validity of his reasoning.

Saint Salvius.

To the same period, the end of the sixth century, belongs the vision of the abbot Salvius, afterwards Bishop of Alby, a close friend of Gregory of Tours, who chronicles the story,[1] and calls God to witness that every word of it is from the very lips of the saint. "On ne contestera pas, je suppose," says Labitte[2] of this vision, "le caractère bien plus céleste qu'infernal des visions sur l'autre monde, durant les premiers âges du christianisme." The comment is perfectly true of the literature with which Labitte is dealing; but he would have qualified his remark considerably had he waded through the fiery rivers of the apocryphal writers.

Gregory's account, considerably condensed, reads as follows. Salvius had been a lawyer of an utterly worldly but stainless life, until, many years before the vision, he took the monastic vows. When the abbot of the monastery died, Salvius was chosen to succeed him; but instead of living a public life, as might have been expected, he retired into greater privacy than before. A fever was the cause of his death, doubtless the result of excessive abstinence and penance. Lying on his bier, he began to move, awoke, red as from sleep, opened his eyes, and stretching out his hands, spoke these words: "O Lord of pity, why hast Thou done this to me,

[1] *Hist. Francorum*, lib. vii. cap. 1.   [2] *Op. cit.*, p. 716.

to permit me to return to this dark place of worldly habitation, when Thy pity in heaven was better for me than the worthless life of this world?" The saint then rose from the bier, and for three days continued without nourishment of any sort. On the third day he made his revelation to the assembled monks. "When you saw me dead four days ago," he said, "and my cell trembled, I was seized by two angels and carried to the heights of heaven, so that I seemed to have under my feet not only this squalid world, but also the sun and moon, clouds and stars." The full text possesses an interest of its own, but space forbids continuous quotation. Briefly, then, the saint was led into a place where was "light unspeakable and unutterable space." The pavement shone like silver and gold, and an innumerable multitude of souls covered it. Following his angel guides through the press, Salvius came under a cloud "brighter than all light," from which came the noise of many waters. From this saluted the saint the martyrs and confessors "in priestly and secular garb." Here also came upon him "an odour of exceeding sweetness," sustained by which, as he explained to the monks, he had lived ever since without other nourishment. Presently he heard a voice saying, "Let this man return to the world, for he is necessary to our Church." At which Salvius, falling on his face on the pavement, said with tears, "Alas, alas! O Lord, why didst Thou show me these things, if I must be thrust out from them? Lo, to-day dost Thou cast me out from Thy face, to return to the perishable world, and no more to be able to return hither." And more in the same strain. The voice replied, "Go in peace. For I am thy Guardian until I bring thee back into this place."

When Salvius has finished his narration, the "odour of sweetness" leaves him, and his tongue swells and festers in his mouth, which makes him fear that he has indiscreetly revealed the mysteries of God. But he avows to God his sincerity of purpose, and evidently obtains relief. The spiritual tone of the vision is manifestly the reflection of the contemplative and devout character of the abbot; and the absence of any mention of sin or punishment in it are the signs of an ascetic remoteness from the world and its affairs.

St. Furseus.

The vision of St. Furseus probably took place about the year 640 A.D. Bede[1] describes him as a "holy man from Ireland," and it is singular that so many of the Purgatory legends should be connected with that country. Furseus was of noble blood, "but much more noble in mind than in birth." He built a monastery in Suffolk, and according to Bede it was there that he had his vision. Wright[2] says, speaking on other authority, that it occurred while he was being carried home to die: in any case he was ill at the time. There

---

[1] *Hist. Eccl.*, lib. iii. cap. 19. Giles' translation.
[2] *Op. cit.*, p. 9.

were really two visions, separated by an interval of two or three days.

In his first vision St. Furseus saw the choirs of angels, and heard them singing " Ibunt sancti de virtute in virtutem: videbitur Deus deorum in Sion." Wright adds one or two details to this, but nothing important.

For full information as to the second and longer vision, Bede refers his readers to a "little book" of the saint's life. This still exists in MSS.,[1] and these have been collected and published in the Bollandist Acts.[2] Bede confines himself to mentioning one or two special features, but his account is quite sufficient for our present purpose.

Lifted up on high by angels, the saint was commanded to look down to earth, and there he saw "as it were a dark and obscure valley underneath him." There were also four fires, hanging in the air near one another, the fires which would some day consume the world: these were unfaithfulness to the promises of baptism, covetousness ("when we prefer the riches of the world to the love of heavenly things"), discord, and lastly the persecution of the weak by robbery or fraud. These fires approach one another, meet and mingle before the eyes of the saint. An angel bids him not to fear when it draws near him: he has not kindled it, and it will not touch him: it is a fire that "tries every man according to the merits of his works." "He also saw devils flying through the fire, raising conflagrations of wars against the

[1] Wright, *op. cit.*, p. 7.   [2] Jan., tom. ii. p. 44.

just." Wright's description of the fires is more pointed, though it is really not different. Each fire is there distinctly said to burn the souls of those who are guilty of the crime which the angel connects with it in his explanation: the crimes are the same.

The saint is then accused by evil spirits, and defended by angels; he is also permitted to discourse with holy men of his own nation long dead, and hears many "salutary" things from them. Returning with his three angel guides to the fire previously mentioned, Furseus had a strange experience. As they were walking through the cleft fire, a devil seized one of the tortured souls and hurled it bodily at the saint, hitting him and leaving burns on his shoulder and jaw, the marks of which he ever afterwards bore. One of the angels instantly returned the soul to the fire, and it then appears that Furseus, on the death of the man whose soul had been flung at him, had received his cloak in payment of some ecclesiastical office or duty. The man had died in his sins, therefore Furseus should not have accepted his money, or rather its equivalent.

Of this vision not very much need be said. The account of the purgatorial fires in Bede's narrative is not very lucid. The fires are, in the end, to burn on the earth and consume all the various sins that are mentioned. Meanwhile they are burning the souls of the wicked, and these will, by inference, be released when the end comes and sin has disappeared. In that sense the fires are purgatorial. The extreme simplicity of the tale is remarkable, and seems to argue that Britain was rather behind the Continent in the development of its ideas upon things infernal.

St. Barontus.

The vision of St. Barontus is mentioned by Wright[1] and Ozanam,[2] and contains a substantial amount of detail. Barontus was, at the time of the vision, a monk in the French "monastery of St. Peter the Apostle, which is called Longoretus," to quote the words of the Bollandists;[3] later he lived the life of a hermit near Pistoria, in Etruria, and, as M. Ozanam puts it, "died for the second time" in the year 685. There is no purpose to be served by repeating the manner of the saint's seizure; suffice it to say that Barontus was smitten with a fever immediately on his return from Matins, and lay in what the Bollandist commentary calls an "extasis immobilis," until the next morning— "manibus ad latus suum extensis et oculis clausis, cepit semivivus jacere, etc. etc." His recovery is no less conventional—"oculos operuit bis terque, laudes Deo redidit, et prima verba hæc ex ore edidit: Gloria tibi Deus: Gloria tibi Deus: Gloria tibi Deus." His ensuing narrative is, briefly, as follows:

As soon as he lay down on his bed, he was overcome by sudden sleep, and instantly two foul demons came to him, and began to strangle him

[1] *Op. cit.*, p. 105.   [2] *Op. cit.*, p. 481.
[3] 25th March (iii. p. 568).

and tear him to pieces, and so take him off to hell. The words of the Latin are strong, for example, "cupientes me efferatis dentibus laniare ac deglutire." This lasted for three hours, and then St. Raphael the Archangel came to his help. In the end the Archangel is successful and carries off the soul of Barontus (anima), leaving his spirit (spiritus) in his body. He touches the monk's throat and his soul comes out of his body, appearing to him to be as small as the newly hatched chick of a little bird. This soul has all the human senses, but it cannot speak until it gets from the air (in some mysterious manner not explained) a body like the one it has just left—"donec ad discussionem veniat, et corpus de aere recipiat, simile ei quod hic reliquit." The incidents of the soul's flight over a monastery, and to a town where the Archangel performs a miracle of healing, may be passed over. Presently the pair are attacked by four more demons, but are rescued by two angels "in veste fulgida et miro odore," who rout the demons and put them all to flight except the original two, who still accompany the saint.

The first gate of Paradise shows Barontus most of the deceased brothers of his own monastery, whom he mentions by name in his narrative. These bewail the fact that the demons have got such an ascendancy over one of their own band, and pray fervently to St. Raphael for the safety of his soul.

At the second gate Barontus finds countless thousands of infants clothed in white and singing praises to God. Further, as they proceed along a tiny path through the midst of the infants, (quaintly called "Sanctorum illorum"), they come upon an innumerable multitude of virgins, who, as soon as they see the saint and his guide, exclaim that a soul is going to judgment, and pray Christ to win it from the devil: "anima ista vadit ad judicium. . . . Tu vince bellator Christe, tu vince: et non diabolus ipsam animam ducat in Tartarum."

Within the third gate, which is like glass, are saints crowned and of shining countenance, dwelling in a splendid mansion and ever giving thanks to God. Priests are here too, those of excellent worth, and their mansions are built with golden bricks and gems ("juxta quod et S. Gregorius in libro Dialogorum commemorat"); there were also many mansions being prepared for dwellers who had not yet appeared, and who are thus described: "qui esurientibus panem in terris tribuere non cessabant."

Next the Holy Martyrs take up the virgins' strain, and so loud is their prayer that Barontus thought it must sound over the whole world. And so they arrived at the fourth gate.

Here the monk who has been commissioned by St. Peter to take charge of all the lights in all the churches of the whole world, chides Barontus for his slackness in the care of his particular lamp. Further than this the saint was not allowed to go in heaven, but he saw (the customary) splendour and brightness which his eyes could hardly bear.

Now Raphael summons St. Peter the Apostle to hear the charges of the demons against Barontus, and to give judgment. This judgment proceeds upon rather peculiar causes, and is worth quoting at some length: " Statim beatissimus Petrus venusto vultu conversus ad ipsos (the demons) dixit: Quod huic monacho habetis crimen imponere? Et dæmones dicerunt, Principalia vitia. Et Petrus dixit: Dicite illa. At illi dicunt: Tres mulieres habuit, quod ei non licuerat: et perpetravit alia vitia, adulteria plurima et alias culpas, quas non ei suasimus; et illa quæ ab infantia gesseram memoraverunt per singula: et hoc quod ego numquam ad memoriam reducebam. Et Petrus ad me ait: Est veritas, frater? Et ego dixi, Veritas, Domine. Et ait ad illos beatus Petrus: Etsi aliquid contrarii egit, eleemosyna redemit: quia eleemosyna a morte liberat: peccata sua Sacerdotibus est confessus, et pœnitentiam pro ipsis peccatis egit: insuper suam comam in meo monasterio deposuit, et omnia propter Deum dereliquit, et semetipsum in servitium Christi tradidit. Omnia ista mala quæ dicitis hæc bona calcaverunt: ideo vos mihi eum auferre non potestis." The demons indignantly protest, but St. Peter finally vanquishes them by threatening to strike them with the keys of heaven. St. Peter proceeds to show Barontus how his salvation is to be completed—namely, by a payment of twelve solidi, in monthly instalments, to the poor! An old man who is standing by, asks if this will really purchase the remission of his sins, and St. Peter repeats himself: "Si hoc quod dici donat statim dimittuntur ei facinora sua. . . . Hoc est pretium divitis et pauperis duodecim solidi." Two little

boys clad in white conduct the saint back to the
first gate, to the souls of his brother-monks who
are to make the necessary arrangements for his
visit to the infernal regions.

Before accompanying him thither, perhaps one
word of comment should be said. It seems not an
unfair inference that St. Barontus' heaven, had he been
permitted to see it all, would have been a sevenfold
one. This traditional scheme becomes less and
less frequent in the Middle Ages, but does occasionally crop up, as for instance in the visions of
Alberic and Tundal, both of the twelfth century.

St. Barontus' hell is rather a slight production:
he was not gifted with much imagination. Passing
over the somewhat lengthy scene in which his escort
is arranged, we come to a vision of Abraham:
"virum senem, pulcherrimum aspectu, habentem
bartam prolixam in alta sede quietum sedentem."
Barontus is now between heaven and hell, and
offers no explanation of Abraham's presence here,
nor of his function, if any he have. The only
comment is quite flat and obvious: ". . . oportet
te semper Dominum rogare, ut cum te a corpore
jusserit migrare, in sinu ipsius Abrahæ te faciat
quietum habitare." When he does arrive in hell,
Barontus finds it difficult to see what is going on
on account of the darkness and smoke. Perhaps
this is his excuse for the total absence of the usual
terrific details of punishment. Here we only find
the sinners bound by demons and groaning with
terror, or likened to bees hurrying into their cells.
Again they are sitting in a circle on leaden seats,

and some stress is laid upon the fact that they are strictly divided into classes: "superbi cum superbis, luxuriosi cum luxuriosis, etc. etc. . . . juxta quod S. Gregorius in libro dialogorum exposuit: Ligabunt eos in fasciculis ad comburendum, et reliqua." Barontus sees a crowd of clerics and some bishops, and, a curious class, virgins who had relied solely on their virginity for merit, and had not added thereto good works. A refreshment is provided every sixth hour for those sinners whose deeds had not been altogether evil: "Omnes illi qui sub custodia dæmonum tenebantur vinculis conligati, et aliqui qui bonum in seculo ex parte egerunt, offerebatur illis hora sexta manna de Paradiso ablatum, similitudinem nebulæ habens, et ponebatur ante eorum nares et ora, et inde refrigerium accipiebant. Similitudinem Levitarum habebant albis vestimentis induti et alii, qui numquam bonum in seculo egerunt, et illis offerebatur: sed gementes oculos suos claudebant, et pectora sua percutiebant, et alta voce dicebant: Væ nobis miseris, qui nullum bonum quod audivimus fecimus, sed et istud tantum malum transactum vidimus."

Finally, to cut a rather wearisome story short, the saint loses the body wherewith, from the air, he has clothed his soul, and is in some danger of failing to accomplish his return to his own proper fleshly abode. However, he is wafted on a miraculous wind, and, entering his body by the mouth, he breaks into his "Gloria tibi Deus."

Drihthelm.

Considerably more elaborate than our previous citation from Bede is the vision of Drihthelm in the year 696, which he recounts in a later chapter of his *Ecclesiastical History*.[1] Drihthelm is described as "a master of a family in that district of the Northumbrians which is called Cuningham, who led a religious life . . ." He fell sick, and died "in the beginning of the night"; the next morning he returned to life, to the consternation of his assembled friends, who all left him and fled, except only his wife. He then divided his property in three equal shares between his wife, his children, and the poor, and spent the rest of his life at the monastery of Melrose, "in such extraordinary contrition of mind and body, that though his tongue had been silent, his life declared that he had seen many things either to be dreaded or coveted, which others knew nothing of."

Like St. Furseus, Drihthelm first beheld a valley: it appeared to lie towards the north-east, and he was led thither silently by an angel with a "shining countenance and a bright garment." Drihthelm's valley, however, is a much more significant place than that of his predecessor. It is very wide and very deep, and of infinite length; on the left it is full of flames, and "the other side was no less horrid for violent hail and cold snow flying in all directions." The "deformed spirits" of the dead

[1] *Op. cit.*, lib. v. cap. 12. See also Othloni, *Liber Visionum*, etc., No. 20; see below, p. 192, note.

MEDIÆVAL LEGENDS 189

leap from one side to the other, seeking in vain some respite from their agony. It is perhaps worth noticing that in other visions where this particular torment occurs, there are often attendant demons armed with hooks to toss the souls from heat to cold and back again. Drihthelm imagines that this place must be hell, "of whose intolerable flames," he quaintly adds, "I had often heard talk." But his guide says he is mistaken, and leaves us to infer that these are the pains of Purgatory.

Hell, however, presently appears, as Drihthelm is led further and further into ever-increasing darkness; it is described as a black abyss from which rise "frequent globes of black flames." These globes contain human souls, and dance on the flames from the abyss, rising when they rise, and when they fail, falling again into the pit. "An insufferable stench" comes from the smoke, and fills the whole air. Drihthelm is here forsaken by his guide, and presently hears dreadful noises behind him: "a most hideous and wretched lamentation, and at the same time a loud laughing, as of a rude multitude insulting captured enemies." And so indeed it is, for he sees demons dragging the howling souls of men into the burning pit. Amongst these souls he distinguished a clergyman, a layman, and a woman. Now Drihthelm is threatened with personal danger, for the fiends come at him with burning tongs; he is rescued, however, by the angel, who reappears shining like a star amid the darkness.

Leaving this place and its gloom, and proceeding to the south-east, Drihthelm and his guide, "in an atmosphere of clear light," come upon a vast wall of boundless height and length, without trace of door or window. Suddenly they are transported, Drihthelm knows not how, to the top of this, and are greeted by an odour of delightful sweetness, which dispels the memory of the "stink of the dark furnace." This fragrance comes from a huge meadow of flowers, in which are "innumerable assemblies of men in white." Again Drihthelm is deceived as to the locality: "This is not," says the angel, "the Kingdom of Heaven, as you imagine."

But, as before, Drihthelm's mistake is immediately demonstrated to him, and he now sees a place which makes the other appear "mean and inconsiderable." The fragrance of heaven he describes as so wonderful that "the other, which I had before thought most delicious, then seemed to me but very indifferent." The light of heaven, too, is much more beautiful, and there are voices heard of souls sweetly singing.

Drihthelm is not allowed to enter this place. The angel suddenly stops, turns, and leads him back to the "joyful mansions of the souls in white," and there, in a delightfully lucid and rational manner, expounds to him the meaning of the things he has seen.

From the facts of the vision, taken along with the statements of the angel, we get a remarkably complete and satisfactory, though not elaborate, system of future punishment and reward, one that commends itself, on the whole, to the modern sense of fitness, perhaps as much as any vision of which an account is given in these pages. The life beyond the grave is here fourfold. First, in Purgatory are the souls of those who repent of their sins at the point of death; "they shall all be received into the kingdom of heaven at the day of judgment," and meanwhile their sufferings can be mitigated "by the prayers, alms, and fasting of the living, and more especially by masses." Second is Hell, "into which whosoever falls shall never be delivered to all eternity," by implication the everlasting abode of the unrepentant. The third state is "that into which the souls of those are received who depart the body in good works, but who are not so perfect as to deserve to be immediately admitted into the kingdom of heaven." Heaven, the last division, is for those who are "perfect in thought, word, and deed."

The most striking feature of the scheme is undoubtedly the third state, the qualified heaven, a sort of blessed purgatory, which is not much less blissful than heaven itself. There is a faint parallel to this in the vision of Tundal, of which an account will be given, and of course, where it occurs, as for instance in the vision of Owain Miles, the earthly paradise represents the same idea. It is a particularly pleasing and rational idea, and probably many will feel that such a classification of souls leaves little to be desired, and is as near to the modern schemes of eschatology as a conception of this early date could well be.

A Letter of St. Boniface.

About the year 730 A.D., a letter was written by St. Boniface to a Saxon abbess called Eadburga, which describes with elaboration a visit to the dead. This letter is contained in the Life of the saint by Willibaldus, and also in a very curious collection of visions, entitled " Liber Visionum tum suarum, tum aliorum Othloni Monachi Sanctemmerammensis Ordinis Sancti Benedicti."[1] The latter book contains twenty-three visions, of which the greater number are quite irrelevant to our subject, and of which the letter to Eadburga is the nineteenth.

The sick man to whom the vision occurred suddenly felt relieved from the heaviness of his body, and, as if casting off the veil of his earthly flesh, he appeared to see the whole world under his gaze. Bright angels receive him and protect him from the fire he presently beholds, by making the sign of the cross, and by laying a hand on his head. He sees innumerable crowds of evil spirits and of good angels disputing for possession of human souls, which are "a huge multitude, more than he had thought there were in the world." His own vices rise up and accuse him in his own voice, as, for instance, " Ego sum cupiditas tua, qua illicita frequentissime et contraria præceptis Dei concupisti"; or, again, " Ego somnolentia qua oppressus tarde ad confitendum Deo surrexisti." The list of his accusers is perhaps sufficiently interesting

[1] Pez, *Thesaurus Anecdotorum Novissimus*, tom. iii. lib. ii. p. 546.

to quote: "vana gloria, mendacium, ociosum verbum quod inaniter locutus fuisti, visus quo videndo illiciter peccasti, contumacia et inobedientia, torpor et desidia, vaga cogitatio et inutilis cura (qua te supra modum sive in Ecclesia sive extra Ecclesiam occupabas) negligentia et incuria, . . . et cætera his similia omnia quæ in diebus vitæ suæ in carne conversatus peregit et confiteri neglexit." Many of these are mere peccadilloes, and some acts or habits which he had never imagined to be sinful "cry out against him terribly." So, too, accuses him the bloody and gaping wound of a man (yet alive) whom in the world he had struck to the effusion of blood. The wound cries out on him, and the blood "ipse propria voce." With becoming modesty is described the answering defence of the good man's virtues: " E contra autem excusantes me clamitabant parvæ virtutes animæ quas ego miser indigne et imperfecte peregi." The demons join in accusing him, while the angels take up his defence.

Hell is quite in the normal style, fiery pits, and the souls hovering in them like black birds. When a soul manages to perch on the edge of a pit for a moment, it means that on the day of judgment it will obtain release. Here, then, we have an admixture of purgatory in hell, but there is another purgatory later in the vision, and most of the souls here are condemned to an eternal fire; for beneath the pits, we read, are terrible groanings which can never be relieved—" ad quas nunquam pia miseratio Domini perveniat."

Heaven is no less traditional. It is a place of wondrous pleasantness, where a great company of beautiful people are playing. There came from it a fragrance of marvellous sweetness, which clothed the blessed spirits who were rejoicing together there: "quem locum sancti angeli affirmabant famosum esse Dei paradisum."

The next section of the vision is important. It describes the bridge with which we are now so familiar, and with which we are not yet done; here a log stretches over a fiery river of boiling pitch, and the souls are hurrying over it to the heavenly Jerusalem, "desiderio ulterioris ripæ." Some get over safely, but many fall into the river, and are more or less immersed in the pitch. Notwithstanding this, however, they reach the other bank far more bright and beautiful than when they fell into the stream. These "needed some slight punishment . . . that they might be worthily offered to God." This is therefore a more real purgatory than the pits of fire mentioned above. The heavenly Jerusalem on the farther bank[1] is only slightly described, and does not appear to be the real heaven of the vision.

One more point must be noticed. The vision contains a system of guardian angels, like that of *The Apocalypse of Paul*, but with a difference. The good have an angel in attendance upon them, while the bad have only a malignant spirit, which

---

[1] Willibaldus reads *citra*, Othlon *circa*, but whatever be the reading, the sense is clear from the phrase "ad quam *post transitum fluminis* festinabant."

suggests a crime to the unfortunate sinner, and then hurries off to hell to announce the deed to its fellows, and so back again to its evil work: "subito apud homines peccata suasit, et ilico apud dæmones perpetrata demonstravit."

The rest of the vision is taken up with special cases of souls in various circumstances, and a somewhat full account of the return of the visitant soul to its body.

Wettin.

Wettin[1] was a monk of the German monastery of Augia, and his vision was taken down at the time from his lips by an ex-abbot of the monastery, by name Hetto. The text here used was discovered in MS. by Baluze, and sent to Mabillon, who printed it in his *Acts*.[2] The same story, almost word for word, is told in a very curious and rare book, of which the British Museum possesses a copy, entitled *Liber trium Virorum et trium Spiritualium Virginum*. This work, by Jacobus Faber, was printed at Paris in 1513, and consists of 190 folii of visions and similar material. At fol. 17 begins the "Libellus de Visione VGVETINI MONACHI."

On a certain Saturday—the year was 824—Wettin, along with his fellow-monks, partook of the apparently customary draught designed to prevent evil effects from the meal which followed—"ad

---

[1] Delepierre, *op. cit.*, p. 43; Labitte, *op. cit.*, p. 719.
[2] "Acta SS. ordinis Sti. Benedicti" (Venice, 1735), tom. iv. pars i. p. 249.

providendam salutem corporis." On this occasion, however, the drink had a very peculiar effect upon Wettin, and on him alone. He at once became very ill ("cœpit magna difficultate indigestam rejicere"), and shrank with disgust from all food. A few days later, his health not being much improved, he had a bed carried for him into a cell only partitioned off from where the other monks were dining, and there lay down and closed his eyes for sleep. Immediately there appeared at his bedside a malign spirit in the shape of a blind clerk, ("in tanta deformitate cæca et tenebrosa facie ut nec signa oculorum in eo apparerent"), with his hands full of instruments of torture. The monk was aghast, but there was worse to come, for the whole room was now filled with similar spirits armed with shields ("scutulis") and spears ("lanceolis"), who set about building a sort of house ("in modum armariorum Italicorum præfiguratum") to shut him in. When Wettin has given up hope of delivery, there suddenly appear angels, who rescue him. He now holds converse with a beautiful angel who appears to him, but the "sermonacio" may be passed over here. The monk then awakes, and relates his experiences to his brethren. The real vision follows, when Wettin goes to sleep again, after having nine or ten folios of the Dialogues of Gregory the Great read aloud to him. The same angel whom he has seen appears to him again, and conducts him to Purgatory. The way is wonderfully bright and pleasant, and from it are seen huge mountains surrounded by a river of fire, in which a countless host of the damned suffer the penalties of sin. Wettin recognised many of these, "innumeris tormentis diversi generis cruciatos," and the first class whose terrible punishment he describes consists of profligate priests, who are bound tightly with thongs in this river of fire, and opposite them, in a similar plight, are the companions of their shame. The angel's comment on the profligacy of the priesthood is not without point—"ita evenit ut nec sibi nec aliis intercessores esse possint."

Wettin's attention is next attracted by a sort of castle, heaped up ("inordinate conjectum") of wood and stone, with smoke rising high from it, the purgatory of certain monks. His guide names one of these who is shut up in a leaden chest as a punishment for some sort of money fraud, in which he had eclipsed Ananias and Sapphira. It appears from the text that this monk had neglected a warning conveyed to him by a similar vision previous to his death.

The angel proceeds to show a lofty mountain, on the summit of which an abbot of ten years ago suffers the pains of Purgatory, which in his case consist of exposure to the continual force of the elements. On another part of the same mountain is a bishop but lately dead, who had neglected to help the abbot by his prayers, as the latter had commanded him in a vision. It appears that the abbot had sent a shade-messenger to the bishop, complaining of the sanitary arrangements of his purgatorial mansion: "dic ei quod præsens mansio mihi et alio data contubernali meo propter hoc sorduit, quia duobus hic comitibus in thermis se lavantibus intolerabilis fœtor inde consurgens, pæne eam nobis inhabitabilem reddidit." The bishop's very apt reply must also be quoted: " Deliramenta, inquit, somniorum non sunt attendenda."

After he has seen a Roman Emperor suffering a dreadful torment, (Charles the Great, as a note explains), Wettin passes to the last punishment of which he has left any record. The worthy monk has got a little out of his depth in his search for a penalty to fit this crime, and what he describes is quite flat and unimpressive. He sees magnificent gifts done up by malignant spirits in cloth of gold and silver and white linen. These are the laws of the counts of the various provinces, and they are thus wrapped up in order that when the counts arrive in hell they may see how justice has been hindered by their bribery and corruption (" muneribus rapinis et avaritia congesta [jura] ").

Then Wettin enters heaven, and sees the throne of Divine Majesty. While he waits, the King of kings and Lord of lords comes forward in a procession of saints. First, the confessors plead for Wettin before the throne, but a voice comes from it, saying, " Exempla ædificationis aliis facere debuit, sed non fecit." Again, the martyrs plead for the forgivenness of his sins, and the voice replies, " Si eos quos male docendo, exemplo suæ pravitatis illexerat, et a via veritatis in viam erroris depravando eos deduxerat, correxerit, et ad viam veritatis reduxerit, remissa sunt." Lastly, the virgins take up the prayer, asking for long life for Wettin, but before they can prostrate themselves the Divine Majesty appears before them, and, raising them, grants their unproffered quest, "Si bona doceat et exempla bona agat, et eos quibus mala præbuit corrigat, erit petitio vestra." It is curious, after this, to read that Wettin awoke convinced of his approaching death, and actually did die on the third evening after the vision.

There are, perhaps, two points worth specially noticing in this story. The first is the appropriateness of penalty and crime, which, though it hardly appears in this short abstract, is quite startling in the original text; and the second point is that the reiterated mention of a certain sordid vice points by an almost unavoidable inference to its unusual prevalence at the time and place of the composition of the story. Apart from these two matters, Wettin's various pictures may be left to speak for themselves.

A certain English Presbyter.

This vision occurs in the second part of the *Annalium Bertinianorum*,[1] under the year 839 A.D., and it is so short and neat that it seems advisable to transcribe the whole story as it stands. Notice that the vision is just a little sermon, devised to point the moral of the loss of the last year's abundant crops, and to constrain the audience to

[1] Perz, *Monumenta Germaniæ Scriptorum*, tom. i. p. 433. ("Auctore Prudentio, Trecensi Episcopo.")

righteousness (and, observe, to almsgiving), by dark hints of worse calamities to come unless they repent, and (quite inconsequently) unless they better observe the Sabbath-day. The picture of boys (the souls of the saints) reading in books in which alternate lines of blood record the sins of men, is not without merit, though the idea strikes no new chord.

"Visio cuiusdam Religiosi Presbyteri de Terra Anglorum Quæ Post Natalem Domini Ei Rapto A Corpore Ostensa Est. Quadam nocte cum idem religiosus presbyter dormiret, quidam homo ad eum venit, præcipiens illi, ut eum sequeretur. Tunc ille surgens, secutus est eum; ductor vero illius duxit eum ad terram sibi ignotam, ubi varia et mira ædificia constructa vidit, inter quæ ecclesia facta erat, in quam ille et ductor eius introivit, ibidemque plurimos pueros legentes videt. Cumque ductorem suum interrogaret, an inquirere auderet, quinam pueri essent, respondit ei: 'Interroga quod vis, et libenter tibi indicabo.' Et cum ad illos appropinquaret, ut videret, quod legerent, perspexit libros eorum non solum nigris litteris, verum etiam sanguineis esse descriptos, ita videlicet, ut una linea nigris esset litteris descripta, et altera sanguineis. Cumque interrogassem,[1] cur libri illi sanguineis lineis descripti essent, respondit ductor meus: 'Lineæ sanguineæ, quas in istis libris conspicis, diversa hominum christianorum peccata sunt, quia ea quæ in libris divinis illis præcepta et iussa sunt, minime facere et adimplere volunt. Pueri vero isti, qui hic quasi legendo discurrunt,

[1] The sudden change to the 1st Person is quaint.

animæ sunt sanctorum, quæ quotidie pro christianorum peccatis et facinoribus deplorant, et pro illis intercedunt, ut tandem aliquando ad pœnitentiam convertantur; et nisi istæ animæ sanctorum tam incessanter cum fletu ad Deum clamarent, iam aliquatenus finis tantorum malorum in christiano populo esset. Recordaris, quia anno præsenti fruges non solum in terra, verum etiam in arboribus et vitibus abundanter ostensæ sunt, sed propter peccata hominum maxima pars illarum periit, quæ ad usum atque utilitatem humanam non pervenit; quod si cito homines christiani de variis vitiis et facinoribus eorum non egerint pœnitentiam, et diem dominicum melius et honorabilius non observaverint, cito super eos maximum et intolerabile periculum veniet; videlicet tribus diebus et noctibus super terram illorum nebula spississima expandetur, et statim homines pagani cum immensa multitudine navium super illos venient, et maximam partem populi et terræ christianorum cum omnibus quæ possident igni ferroque devastabunt. Sed tamen, si adhuc veram pœnitentiam agere volunt, et peccata illorum iuxta præceptum Domini ieiunio et oratione atque eleemosynis emendare studuerint, tunc has pœnas et pericula per intercessionem sanctorum evadere poterunt.'"

St. Anschar.

The life of St. Anschar[1] has been written in verse by Gualdo, and in prose by Rembertus; both

[1] Delepierre, *op. cit.*, p. 47.

versions are printed in Langebek's *Scriptores Rerum Danicarum Medii Ævi*.[1] St. Anschar was born in Picardy in September 801, and entered the monastery of Corbeia there in his thirteenth year. He died in 865, the first archbishop of Hamburg, and was succeeded by his biographer, St. Rembertus.

When he was a mere baby of five, it appears that Anschar was guilty of a certain puerile levity of character. He was more fond of joking with companions of his own age than of studying to discipline himself. To correct this reprehensible tendency, a vision was vouchsafed to him, in which the Virgin Mary enjoined upon him, so to speak, a seriousness of purpose more fitted to his years: "si nostræ societatis particeps esse volueris, omnem debes vanitatem fugere, et jocos pueriles dimittere; valde enim nos detestamur omnia, quæ vana et otiosa sunt; nec potest in nostro conventu esse, quicunque fuerit hisce delectatus."

Chiefly as a result of this vision, Anschar from that time forward devoted himself to reading and meditation (please remember that he was five years old!), and shunned all "puerilia consortia." The death of Charles the Great in 814 made a great impression on the youthful monk, and he devoted himself with the utmost rigour to abstinence and watching, so that, to quote again, " . . . his virtutum exercitiis verus Athleta Domini insisteret, atque in hac gravitate permanenti mortuus illi mundus fieret, et ipse mundo." The main vision occurred at Pentecost of this same year, and is attributed by

[1] Tom. i. pp. 427 *seq.* and 561 *seq.*

the biographer to the working of the same grace of the Holy Spirit which was once poured out upon the apostles at that season. St. Anschar suddenly felt that he was going to die, and in the very article of death he called upon St. Peter the Apostle and the blessed St. John the Baptist, who immediately appeared to him, just as his soul seemed to leave his body and enter another very beauteous body which lacked all appearance of mortality. The descriptions of the saints are not quite conventional, and therefore perhaps worth quoting. "Quorum unus erat senior, cano capite, capillo plano et spisso, facie rubenti, vultu subtristi, veste candida et colorata, statura brevi, quem ipse S. Petrum esse, nemine narrante, statim cognovit. Alius vero juvenis erat statura procerior, barbam emittens, capite subfusco atque subcrispo, facie macilenta, vultu jocundo, in veste serica, quem ille S. Johannem omnino credidit."

St. Anschar's soul finds itself in a vast brightness which fills all the world, and his guides lead him through this to a place which, "nemine narrante," he instantly recognises as Purgatory. Here St. John and St. Peter leave him, and he suffers terrible darkness and pressures and suffocations, and is so dreadfully distressed thereby that his memory fails him, and his only thought is how there can possibly be such an awful punishment—"hæc solum excogitare sufficiebat, quomodo tam immanis possit existere pœna." When he has been here for three days as he thinks, which seemed longer than a thousand years, the saints reappear, and lead him, with far greater alacrity and joy than before, and through an if possible greater brightness, to heaven. From this point the vision is related in the *ipsissima verba* of the visionary. " I saw," he says, " from afar the various ranks of saints, some standing nearer to the east, and some further off, but all looking towards the east. And all were adoring Him Himself who appeared in the east, praising Him together with hands stretched out, some with bowed heads, and some with faces bent down." And then, when he and his guides had reached " the east," St. Anschar saw the four and twenty elders of St. John's Apocalypse, sitting in seats, and they too are reverently looking eastwards, uttering ineffable praises to God. Their song gave Anschar great refreshment at the time, but when he came back to the body he could in no wise remember it. Then follows a somewhat full description of the " claritas " of the place, which is of every colour, and from it the souls of the saints who inhabit the place drink gladness. Round those who are seated it takes the form of a rainbow. It emanates from Jesus, (though the reading here is perhaps not quite certain), with this comment—" de quo Petrus ait: in quem desiderant Angeli prospicere." It is, however, not such a light as to inconvenience the eyes of beholders, but rather most pleasantly to satiate them. One significant phrase, too seldom found in these descriptions, states the non-material nature of everything which St. Anschar saw: " nam nihil corporeum erat ibi, sed erant cuncta incorporea, licet speciem corporum habentia, et ideo ineffabilia." In this place, in a word, St. Anschar (" nemine monstrante ") realises that there resides the Majesty of God Omnipotent, and presently a voice of great sweetness comes to him from this Majesty, saying " Vade, et ad me revertere [martyrio coronatus [1]]." And the saints held silence and adored God with bowed heads. Let the saint now finish his own story. " And after this voice I became sad, because I was compelled to go back to the world, but sure in the promise of return, I departed thence with my guides. And they spoke not at all with me going nor coming, but for their affection they looked upon me as a mother gazes at her only son. And so I came to my body. And neither in going nor returning was there any toil nor delay, because we were instantly at the place whither we were aiming. And although I have seemed to tell of so great sweetness of sweetnesses, yet I confess that in vain has my pen striven to express things so high as my mind felt, and neither did my mind feel as the thing really was: for it seemed to me to be what eye hath not seen, nor ear heard, nor has it entered into the heart of man."

Bernold.

The vision of the presbyter Bernold, a parishioner of Hincmar,[2] Archbishop of Rheims about the middle of the ninth century, related by the latter

[1] The suggested addition of another text.
[2] *Opera*, tom. ii. ("Opuscula et Epistolæ"), p. 805.

in a letter to his clergy, is in one respect quite a Divine Comedy in miniature. Whether there is some basis of fact in it or no, it is, of course, impossible to say, but it is practically a vehicle for Hincmar's criticisms of his lately deceased Emperor, and his defeated rival for the episcopal chair. But here the resemblance ceases: the vision is of little eschatological moment. The preliminaries are quite as usual, and may therefore be omitted. Bernold first arrives at a place where he finds forty-one bishops, amongst whom he recognises certain, (with whom we must suppose that Hincmar had had some difference of opinion). They are clad in rags, and blackened as if they had been burnt, and filthy, and they chatter their teeth with cold and boil with heat in turn. ". . . per vices nimio frigore horribiliter cum fletu et stridore dentium tremulantes, et per vices calore nimio æstuantes." The bishops send Bernold with a guide to another place, where he finds their people, clergy and laity, and by asking for their prayers for the bishops, Bernold is able to obtain for them some relief.

Next Bernold finds the Emperor Charles the Bald, lying in putrefaction and eaten of worms, in a place which is dark, but whither light penetrates from a neighbouring part which is described as most clean, and beautifully flowery, and sweet-smelling. " Et vidi ibi iacere domnum nostrum Karolum regem in luto ex sanie ipsius putredinis, et manducabant eum vermes, et jam carnem illius manducatam habebant et non erat in corpore ipsius aliud

MEDIÆVAL LEGENDS

nisi nervi et ossa." At the Emperor's request, Bernold puts a stone under his head, and receives a message for Hincmar that Charles is suffering his present torment because he did not pay heed to the admonitions of the bishop. He is, further, enjoined to ask for prayers for the Emperor's liberation from his faithful people.

The Emperor explains that the place of light and fragrance is the Rest of the Saints—" Sanctorum requies," and Bernold pushes on thither through the usual sweetness and brightness which human tongue cannot tell. Bernold's heaven is no heaven at all. He finds Hincmar there, robed for mass, and gives him Charles' message. Immediately he returned to where he had seen Charles, and found that already his condition was very much improved!

But the vision is not worth pursuing in detail. Bernold obtains the relief of two other individual souls in a similar way, and he sees the punishment of souls *en masse*, carried out in a smoky well or pit by demons with such familiar accessories as flames and icy cold water. The doctrine of the efficacy of masses, prayers, and alms for the relief of the dead in Purgatory is the predominant moral of the vision, such as it is.

There is a little dispute between a good and bad spirit about the length of Bernold's life and the ultimate destiny of his soul, which is not without interest, and suggests comparison with several similar scenes already noticed. These two spirits are quaintly described: one is "homo valde honestus," the other "homo rustica facie et tortuo vultu." Bernold has a staunch champion in the person of his good angel, confident of victory: "Sic erit sicut ego dico non sicut tu, quia ecce hic est suus advocatus et fideiussor, et tu eris ibi mecum."

The Emperor Charles III.

Charles III became Emperor in the year 875. His vision is told by William of Malmesbury,[1] from whose version the following Latin quotations are taken; those in English are from the translation of the same work by the Rev. John Sharpe.[2] Charles, then, was "rapt in the spirit," and that by a guide most glorious to behold, who held in his hand a thread which gave a wonderful light; this Charles had to tie to his thumb, and thus secure of his return, a later Theseus, he proceeded to plumb the depths of hell: "labyrintheas infernorum poenas." First, deep and fiery valleys, where are the bishops of Charles' father and uncles, confined in pits boiling with pitch, brimstone, lead, wax, and grease. This punishment they endure as "sowers of discord" and "fomenters of evil," and they inform Charles that they are expecting his bishops and ministers to join their number. Then black demons attempt to seize with their fiery claws the thread which

---

[1] § 111 (which is lib. ii. § 6), *Rerum Britannicarum Medii Ævi Scriptores*, vol. i. p. 112. William takes the vision from Hariulf, *Chronicon Centulense*, lib. iii.

[2] London, 1815.

Charles holds, but they are beaten off by the rays which strike from the ball. When the fiends attempt to seize the Emperor himself, his guide throws a loop of the thread over his shoulders, and thus drags him onwards. Now they come to a region of fiery mountains and marshes and blazing rivers, and all kinds of metals boiling, where Charles sees immersed countless souls of his own and his family's vassal princes, some up to the hair, some to the chin, some to the navel; these had loved battle and slaughter and rapine, "pro cupiditate terrena." One touch here should not be missed. The vision is plainly intended as a warning to Charles himself, and the sinners therefore associate themselves with Charles and his family. "Dum viximus, amavimus tecum, et cum patre tuo, et cum fratribus tuis, et cum avunculis tuis, facere prælia, . . ."

There is nothing strikingly original about the next section of the vision — furnaces of boiling pitch and sulphur, full of dragons and scorpions and serpents of various sorts. These contain other princes, who confess to malice and pride, and evil counsel given to Charles and their other rulers for greed's sake. Charles is protected from the serpents by a triple fold of the thread. Next they came down into a valley which was dark and burning on one side, but on the other indescribably pleasant and glorious. On the dark side Charles sees some kings of his own race suffering great punishment, and thought he was about to be plunged into the same by some terrific giants who filled the valley with all sorts of fire and flame. He then sees two springs, one boiling hot, the other clear and warm, issue from the side of the valley and fill two casks standing there. This is the purgatory of his father Lewis, who spends his days in the casks alternately. He asks for the prayers and alms of his son, of his faithful bishops and abbots, and of the whole ecclesiastical order.

Lewis then proceeds to show his son a couple of boiling casks reserved for *his* future entertainment: "nisi te emendaveris et pœnitentiam egeris de tuis nefandis delictis." Seeing that Charles was in a great state of fear, his guide now led him to the other side of the valley, which is described as Paradise—"ad dextram luculentissimæ vallis paradisi." Here is his uncle Lothaire, sitting in the company of other kings, on an enormous topaz, and crowned with a precious diadem, and near him his son Lewis, similarly adorned. These conversed with Charles about other matters—his father's punishment, his own approaching death, and especially about the succession to the empire; and an infant appears, who is also a Lewis, the grandson of the last, and into whose hand Charles delivers the thread of light which he holds, as a token that the Imperial power is one day to be his. "Thus, after this wonderful transaction, my spirit, extremely wearied and affrighted, returned into my body. Therefore let all persons know, willingly or unwillingly, forasmuch as, according to the will of God, the whole empire of the Romans will revert into his hands, and that I cannot prevail against him, compelled by the condition of this my calling, that God, who is the ruler of the living and the dead, will both complete and establish this; whose eternal kingdom remains for ever and ever. Amen." The conclusion of the story seems to have a distinctly political object.

Walkelin (Galchelmus).

This vision of a priest of Bonneval, a village in the diocese of Lisieux, is told by Ordericus Vitalis,[1] and assigned to the year 1091. It is of some little length, but it is not necessary to do more than give a brief series of the pictures of dooms which Walkelin saw. The vision begins quite suddenly by the priest finding himself surrounded by a troop of cavalry when he was pursuing his solitary way homewards by moonlight. A giant armed with a club figures in this scene. Presently there comes upon the astonished gaze of Walkelin a most extraordinary procession. First, a wailing crowd of pedestrians, some of them known to the priest, carrying cattle ("pecudes") and clothes and all sorts of furniture and utensils on their necks and shoulders: "Quæ prædones asportare solent." Next, a troop of corpse-bearers carrying on their fifty biers men of the size of dwarfs, but with heads as big as barrels. Then came two Ethiopians carrying a tree-trunk, to which was bound an un-

[1] *Historia Ecclesiastica*, pars iii. lib. viii. cap. 17 (Migne, *Patrologiæ Cursus Completus*, tom. 188, col. 607). I have also used Bohn's translation (Thomas Forester), vol. ii. p. 511.

fortunate, whom Walkelin recognises as the assassin of a certain priest called Stephen; and a demon sat on the trunk and goaded the criminal's back and loins with fiery spurs till the blood ran.

Now comes a countless band of women riding on side-saddles, in which are fixed glowing nails, and the wind lifts them "as it were a cubit" off the saddle, and lets them drop again on the burning points. "Woe! Woe!" they cry, and openly confess the sins for which they are paying such a penalty. Even amongst these carnal sinners the priest recognises several, and, what is more strange, he sees their "palfreys and mules" ready for some known to him who are still alive. The only noteworthy point about the "company of clergy" which now tails past is that Walkelin recognised many "who, in human estimation, were now associated with the saints in heaven." But, as Orderic has it, "Humanus plerumque fallitur intuitus, sed Dei medullitus prospicit oculus. Homo enim videt in facie, Deus autem in corde. . . . nihil inquinatum illuc intromittitur. Nihil sordidum, honestatique contrarium, illic reperitur. Unde quidquid inconveniens fæx carnalis commisit, purgatorio igne decoquitur, variisque purgationibus, prout æternus censor disponit, emundatur."

An immense army now passes the priest, mounted on coal-black steeds, and there was no colour at all in the army, only blackness and flame. Walkelin, desiring to take away with him some testimony to the truth of his story, tries to seize a horse, (for some follow riderless). The first he grasps escapes him, but he is preparing to mount a second when he feels that the stirrup is red-hot iron, while the hand that holds the bridle is frozen stiff. The horse itself blows a cloud from its nostrils as big as the biggest oak.

Four knights now ride up breathing out threats upon the would-be horse-thief. One of them begs Walkelin to deliver a message to his wife, and incidentally relates his curious history. He had received a mill as security from a poor debtor, and had left this to his own heirs, to the exclusion of the mortgagee's kin. For this harshness he is compelled to carry a glowing lump of iron from the mill in his mouth, "which I feel," he adds, "to be more oppressive than the tower of Rouen." He requests Walkelin, then, to see that the property is restored, that his soul may have peace. When the priest refuses, the knight seizes him by the throat with a hand that burns like fire, and drags him along the ground, with threats.

Walkelin is rescued from this predicament by a knight, who turns out to be his brother, and with whom he has considerable talk. There is but one more point of detail to be noticed, namely, a mass of clotted blood like the head of a man clinging about the spurs of the priest's brother. The latter explains that it is not blood but fire, and that the weight of it is intolerable; it is a punishment for using bright spurs on earth to hurry after blood. "Et quia pretiosis et acutis utebar calcaribus ut festinarem ad effundendum sanguinem, jure sarcinam in talis bajulo enormem; qua intolerabiliter gravatus, nulli hominum exprimere valeo pœnæ quantitatem. Hæc indesinenter meditari mortales deberent, et timere, imo cavere, ne pro reatibus suis tam dira luerent."

The Icelandic "Song of the Sun."

About the year 1100 A.D., Sæmund, the son of Sigfus, an Icelander by birth, is supposed to have collected those poems of his native land which are now known as the Elder or Poetic Edda. Amongst these there is one, the "Song of the Sun," which relates a vision of heaven and hell, and which, besides, contains Christian elements. As Sæmund spent a considerable time on the continent of Europe, and studied in French and German universities,[1] this latter is not remarkable, still less when we reflect that the Christian religion had been legally established in Iceland some fifty years before the date mentioned.[2] The "Song of the Sun" is indeed, however, very incongruous with its setting. It is buried deep in pagan mythology, in those splendid old sounding tales of the Scandinavian gods and heroes which still make the blood run faster; while itself, at least the part of it which is here relevant, is far nearer akin to the class of visions which we have just left, and to which we shall presently return. On the whole, it seems very possible that the vision is at any rate in part the work of the collector, or of his period. There is

[1] Mallet's *Northern Antiquities* (Bohn), p. 363.
[2] *The Edda of Sæmund* (Benjamin Thorpe), Preface.

nothing in older Icelandic literature to parallel it, and so much in Christian literature. But, needless to say, that is a question for an expert to decide; it may be added that some of the MSS. of the poem actually do assign it to Sæmund.[1]

The "Song of the Sun" is a poem of 83 strophes or 496 lines, but only a short half of these are concerned with the experience of the soul amongst the dead. A comparison of Thorpe's translation with the rendering which Wright gives in his Appendix results so much in favour of the latter, that it is preferred in this place. It does not seem necessary to apologise for the length of the quotation; it is undeniably of great interest, and a mere summary of its contents would be monotonous, and very long in proportion. The alignment of Wright's translation has been sacrificed for the sake of brevity, but the loss is trifling.

"In the Norni's seat sat I nine days; thence I was carried on a horse; the sun of the Gygiars shone grimly out of the apertures of the clouds. Without and within I seemed to go through all the seven lower worlds; above and below sought I a better way, where I might have a more agreeable journey. I must relate what I first saw, when I was come into the places of torment—scorched birds,[2] which were souls, fled numerous as flies. From the west saw I fly the dragons of expectation, and open the way of the fire-powerful; they beat their wings, so that everywhere it appeared to me that earth and heaven burst. The sun's hart

[1] Thorpe, *op. cit.*, pt. i. p. 117.   [2] Cf. above, p. 193.

I saw go from the south, him led two together: his feet stood on the ground, and his horns touched heaven. From the north saw I ride the people's sons, and they were seven together; with full horns they drank the pure mead from the fountain of heaven's lord. The wind became quiet, the waters ceased to flow; then heard I a fearful sound: for their husbands, shameless women ground earth to food. Bloody stones those dark women dragged sorrowfully; their bleeding hearts hung out of their breasts, weary with much grief. Many men saw I wounded go in the ways strewed with hot cinders; their faces seemed to me all to be red with smoking blood. Many men saw I go on the ground who had been unable to obtain the Lord's meal; heathen stars stood over their heads, painted with fearful characters. Those men saw I who cherish much envy at others' fortune; bloody runes were on their breasts marked painfully. Men saw I there many, without joy, who all wandered pathless; that he purchases for himself, who of this world is infatuated with the vices. Those men saw I who in many ways laid their hands on others' property; they went in flocks to Fegiarn's (Satan's) city, and had burthens of lead. Those men saw I who many had deprived of money and life; through their breasts suddenly pierced strong venomous dragons. Those men saw I who would not keep holy days; their hands were on hot stones nailed tight. Those men saw I who in much pride magnified themselves too much; their garments were in derision with fire surrounded. Those men saw I who had many words against another lied; hell's ravens out of their heads cruelly tore their eyes. All the horrors you cannot know which the hell-goers have. Sweet sins go to cruel recompenses; ever cometh moan after pleasure. Those men saw I who much had given according to God's laws; clear candles were over their heads burning brightly. Those men saw I who magnanimously improved the condition of the poor; angels read the holy books over their heads. Those men saw I who had much their body lean with fasting; God's angels bowed before all these; that is the greatest pleasure. Those men saw I who to their mother had put food in the mouth; their resting-places were in the beams of heaven placed agreeably. Holy virgins had purely washed the soul of sins, of those men who many a day punish themselves. Lofty cars I saw go midst heaven, which had the roads to God; men guide them who were slain entirely without fault. O mighty Father, most great Son, Holy Ghost of heaven, I pray thee to save (who didst create) us all from miseries!"

Alberic.

An account is now to be given of several visions of the twelfth century, which represent, as it were, the fully developed tradition of Heaven, Purgatory, and Hell. It will be sufficiently obvious, without calling attention to individual details, that these works have gathered to themselves the significant features of previous legends, and it will surely be acknowledged that they have done so in a manner that deserves praise. Further, they are bound to suggest, by their multiplicity of detail, collected, as it were, from past ages, that there is not much room left, after them, for originality or invention. It is still a common opinion that one of the chief wonders of Dante's genius is his unlimited fertility of imagination in the region of the horrible. How far from the truth such an opinion is, the evidence of literary history undoubtedly proves. It is Dante's manner that demands our praise, his ennobling treatment of material which in other hands was often vulgar, often meaningless, and often merely grotesque.

The vision of the boy Alberic has this special interest for students of Dante, that it owes its notoriety largely to the fact that the poet was once accused of copying it to a large extent. The matter has already been noticed in the Introduction to this Essay; it is mentioned again in order to state that it is from Cancellieri's work [1] that the following account is taken. He has printed the Latin text in full, with a parallel Italian translation. The vision dates from the beginning of the twelfth century.[2]

When the guileless prologue informs us that the vision was revealed to a boy of nine years, we are perfectly prepared for the elaborate and highly artificial catena of prodigies which follows. But the story

[1] *Osservazioni sopra l'Originalità della Divina Commedia di Dante.* Francesco Cancellieri, Rome, 1814.
[2] Labitte, *op. cit.*, p. 728.

is itself so long that comment must be cut short; and indeed the work does not provoke much in the way of either admiration or criticism. It is a palpable conglomeration of the ideas of its predecessors, something altered here and added there, but it is worth close attention, for the reason that it is, in its Purgatory, more complete than any other vision here recorded. It is the first really comprehensive vision, indeed, which has come under review in this chapter.

The precocious Alberic was the son of a Campanian noble, lord of the castle of " Sette Fratelli," and at the early age which has been mentioned was smitten one day with a grievous sickness, and lay for nine days like dead. His manner of introduction to the realms of the dead during this trance is as follows: A white bird like a dove puts its beak in his mouth, and he feels he knows not what to be taken out therefrom. The bird then lifts him off the ground as much as a man's height, and thereafter appear to him the blessed Apostle Peter and two angels, called Emmanuel and Helos; thus escorted, he visits the places of punishment and of hell.

First are the souls of infants of a year in raging flame and vapour of fire, for the pains of Purgatory run parallel with the age of man, as the apostle explains, waxing with his strength and waning with his decline. St. Peter is careful to explain that not even an infant of a day dies sinless; even such are liable to the " accidents of human frailty." Therefore infants of one year are cleansed in this fire for seven days, of two years for fourteen days, and so on. Enough has been said on this subject elsewhere.[1]

Next the boy is led to a terrible valley, full of beings frozen into tall columns of ice, which not only freeze but burn the wretched souls thus immured. These are the adulterous and unchaste, and some are buried up to the ankles, some to the knees or thighs, some to the breast, and others totally submerged, according to the degree of their crime.

In another more terrible valley there are women hanging by their pierced breasts on the sharp branches of great trees, while two serpents suck the breasts of each. These have refused sustenance to their foster-children. Other women, who have broken their marriage vow, hang by the hair in burning flames.

The next torment of Alberic's story takes an interesting and familiar form—an iron ladder, blazing and shooting sparks, stretching upwards from a huge pot of boiling oil and pitch and resin. The sinners of this Purgatory are compelled to essay the ascent, with scorched feet, a worse fate awaiting them if they fall into the pot below. These are married persons of uncontrolled passions. The section concludes by explaining that all sinners do not suffer all the penalties, for each sin has its proper pain.

Tyrants and murderers of their children (" mulieres pessimæ quæ suos interficiunt antequam nascantur filios ") are punished in balls of sulphurous flame. The children of the latter class appear before them, and testify against them. In spite of his extreme

[1] See above, pp. 53, 54.

youth, was Alberic acquainted with the apocryphal apocalypses?[1]

A fire, with all the appearance of a lake of blood, burns the souls of homicides, each of whom, for three years, must carry hung from his neck an evil spirit in the shape of his victim. Afterwards he is plunged into this fire.

Alberic next approaches an enormous vessel full of boiling brass, tin, lead, sulphur, and resin, one end of which is held by a huge horse of fire. Through an opening in the other end creep in the blood-stained souls of those who have connived at or ignored the wickedness of their priests. A bishop guilty of the same laxity towards a presbyter is doomed to eighty years of this torment instead of the normal three years. The only way out of the fire is through the belly of the blazing horse.

The following section deals with hell and the mouth of the infernal pit ("loca tartarea, . . . os infernalis baratri"). It appears like a well full of darkness and horror and stench and shriekings, and the guardian of the spot is a vast worm fastened with a chain, one end of which seems to be secured in hell. "Before the mouth of the worm stood a crowd of souls, all of whom he drew in at once like flies, for when he drew breath he swallowed them all at once, and when he let out his breath he put them all out again burnt up like sparks." The writer does not fail to quote the obvious verse from Isaiah in support of the truth of this punishment.

[1] See above, pp. 130, 149.

The darkness here is so great that Alberic can see nothing very clearly; he is told, however, that those who are in hell have no judgment, but perish without it, which seems, to say the least of it, a little self-contradictory. How did the souls in hell get there?

Liquid metal is the penalty appropriate to sacrilege, and there is nothing striking about the pains attached to simony. A place whose description is not unlike that of the mouth of hell, excepting the worm, is reserved for those who renounce their religious vows and go back into the world, or who have repented of their sins, but not brought forth the fruits of repentance. Here such souls are cleansed of their dross, as gold in a furnace is refined and sheds all its alloy.

In a foul sulphurous lake, full of serpents and scorpions, are immersed slanderers and false witnesses. On the shores stand demons armed with whips of snakes, with which they lash the mouths and faces and heads of those poor sinners.

Now Alberic is to see the directing genii of the place. All the pains of Purgatory are governed by two evil spirits, in the likeness of a dog and of a lion, belching fire and sulphurous breath, with a blast of which they hurl each soul to its allotted doom, as a whirlwind sweeps the dust from the face of the earth (". . . . ipso sui flatus impulsu in quamlibet penam impingebant, velut cum turbo vehemens proiicit pulverem a facie terre."

Here Alberic is left for a moment by the apostle, hard by the barriers of hell, and is terrified by the hostile approach of one of the demons, but St. Peter returns before harm is done. He then witnesses the punishment of thieves and rapacious persons, who wear blazing chains on their bare flesh, shooting sparks like iron new from the furnace. These are fastened to their hands, their feet, and their throats, and to the last weights are attached, so heavy that the poor wretches cannot stand erect.

The next Purgatory is important, containing as it does a feature which is common to many schemes of the future life, and to which special attention has already been drawn. Here, then, Alberic sees a mighty river of pitch proceeding from hell, and over it stretches a bridge of iron, broad when the just are crossing, but contracting to a thread when a sinner reaches the middle of it, and plunging the unlucky wretch, weighed down by his guilt, into the depths below. There in the boiling pitch the sin-stained souls are gradually purged (" in morem carnium excocti ") until they succeed in effecting the passage of the bridge. The apostle's "nil desperandum," and his anecdote in support thereof, need not be recorded.

St. Peter now shows the boy a vast plain covered so thick with thorns and thistles that there is no room to set one's foot. Here a devil mounted on a dragon is chasing souls, and beating them with a serpent which he brandishes as often as he overtakes them. Each soul, however, becomes gradually lightened of its load of sin, and ultimately effects its escape into another most pleasant plain, where its garments and its limbs are alike restored, and it is welcomed by the souls of the just, who return thanks to God for the delivery of each newcomer. This plain is described in quite conventional terms: there is the customary fragrance of flowers, and no tongue can tell of the beauty and glory of the scene. In the middle of the plain is Paradise, ("paradisus" simply), into which the souls of the just may not enter until the day of judgment.

At this point the reader of the Latin text must infallibly discover, if he knew it not before, that the vision is the product of a monastery. As a matter of fact, Alberic describes himself in his prologue as "Casinensis cenobii Monachus," and relates how he has revised his own vision and given it the shape which he desires to be permanent. But even without this information the monkish hand is betrayed, for, with hardly an exception, the remaining sections of the book are written in the regular style of the monastery: words of counsel to monks are put into St. Peter's mouth, and there is a deal about the glory of the ascetic life and its final reward in heaven. There are a few further points of interest, however. Paradise is guarded by cherubim, and in it are the tree of life and the tree whereof Adam tasted. The only saints whom St. Peter mentioned as already dwelling there are Abel, Abraham, Lazarus, and the penitent thief, which seems rather an arbitrary selection. Alberic is forbidden to say who was lying on a couch hard by attended by four priests in sacred garments, just as he is prohibited from disclosing what he

MEDIÆVAL LEGENDS

saw in a certain place enclosed by high walls. This is an obvious and frequent device.

Lastly may be mentioned a sevenfold scheme of heavens,[1] which has for some time been absent from these pages. Nothing is made of the idea here; in fact, with the exception of the barest word or two of astronomy, the heavens are only named in their order. In the seventh heaven, for instance, is the star Saturn, which gives its heat and splendour to the sun! In this highest heaven is the throne of God, and the six-winged cherubim always standing before the glory of His majesty do not cease to cry, "Holy, holy, holy, Lord God of Sabbaoth."

Alberic is afterwards conducted through the fifty-one provinces, of which he faithfully gives a list, and he witnesses amongst others an extraordinary purgatorial scene in a ruined church in a deserted city. The details of this need not be reproduced here, as there is nothing very noticeable in them. Two points do, however, call for remark. The first is an indication that a good deed, and especially a charitable action, done on earth, may ease a tortured soul after death. This recalls the case of Judas in the voyage of Brandan.[2] The other matter is that, as Wright[3] observes, these last torments are witnessed by Alberic in various parts of this earth. Strangely enough, this too reminds us of Judas on his sea-girt rock, and of the story of the soul in the block of ice, to which reference was there made.

[1] See above, pp. 104, 105.   [2] See above, p. 167, and note.
[3] *Op. cit.*, p. 121.

The Child William.

This age appears to have been prolific of infant precocity. The story of the child William is told by Vincent of Beauvais under the year 1146, and his "Cronographus" adds the note that a boy of the same name was crucified by the Jews in Norwich on the Day of Preparation for the Passover in that year. A shining man appeared to the hero of the story—who was fifteen years of age—and bade him follow. They arrive at a dark valley with fire on one side and cold water on the other, between which torments souls are constantly passing. Next enormous chairs of fire, filled with a countless host of people, with demons at hand torturing them by putting blazing coins into their mouths— "dæmones monetam flammeam de sacculis proferebant, et in ora singulorum projiciebant, quam illi per voces et guttur emittebant; sed dæmones iterum in ora eorum reinferebant." Afterwards the child saw bodies which seemed to have the shape of full-grown men thrown into cauldrons where they immediately became like new-born babes. Pulled out of the cauldrons on blazing forks, they were immediately transformed to their former age. Again, in another fire, the members all come away from one another, but are joined together again when the bodies are hauled out. Next he saw men and women fixed to revolving wheels, and calling out in their agony. Others he sees hanging head downwards over fire, others perishing with cold with garments under them which they could not reach, others starving with food just beyond their grasp. The following sentence is well worth attention, though not peculiar to this vision : " Et in quacumque necessitate positis aliis non subvenerant, in eadem consolationem nullam recipiebant." Afterwards the child saw Tartarus opened, and its depth seemed to him greater than is the road from Dorobernia to Londonia! And there, in hell, sat the "ancient enemy" stretched out " in sex partes." While the boy stood trembling at the mouth of the pit, a foul demon, which had all the time accompanied him on his left side, began to accuse him. He silences it, however, and puts it to flight with the sign of the Cross. His guide leaves him alone trembling in the darkness for a time, but soon returns and leads him to heaven.

In a great brightness they come to a wall of infinite length and width—a detail which is already familiar and will recur. There is no opening in the wall, but in a moment they are wafted over it, and see a round house with twelve doors, " ut scriptum est : Ab oriente portæ tres, etc." Entering this, William saw that it was so vast that all things in the world would not fill a tenth part of it, and there he saw many in great glory, but not all in equal glory, and ten bands of the blessed (dead). In the eastern part they find another group of glorious persons sitting, and all regard one of their number as the chief. His guide's explanation is as follows : " Hic tibi locus si bene vixeris, sciasque hunc eose puerum Guillelmum quem Judæi apud Norunicum crucifixerunt."

Tundal.

This vision is one of the fullest and most elaborate which exist, and has attracted a great amount of attention from bibliographers. Written in Latin,[1] it was translated into several languages, and printed as early as 1473. The date was 1149, previous to the descent of Owain into St. Patrick's Purgatory; it is an important feature in the story that Tundal, like the visitors to the Irish cave, was himself obliged to undergo pains and torments during his sojourn with the dead. Delepierre[2] attaches the highest importance to Tundal's story: "Par ses détails, c'est une autre 'Divine Comédie' en prose." As to the date, this writer agrees with the year mentioned, and cites the quaint parenthesis of an old literary history:[3] "Stephano rege in Anglia dominante, et Satana apud Hybernos suas vires exercente." Delepierre tells the tale from a Latin MS. of the fourteenth century, which he had previously translated for the first time into French for the " Société des Bibliophiles de Mons." This translation, a very pretty book printed in red, green, and blue ink, is to be found in the British Museum, but not easily elsewhere. Of nearly equal rarity is the text which it is now proposed to summarise. In 1843, W. B. D. D. Turnbull, a member of the Scottish Bar, published 105 copies of a selection from a MS.[4] of the fifteenth century,

---

[1] A good text is that of Oscar Schade, *Visio Tnugdali*, Halis Saxonum, 1869.   [2] *Op. cit.*, p. 63 *seq.*

[3] Balæus, cent. xiv.   [4] He gives the number as Jac. v. 7, 27.

in the Advocates' Library at Edinburgh, of which the vision of Tundal forms a considerable part. Mr. Turnbull's introduction contains a notice of the more interesting early printed editions of the vision. The title of his edition is "The Visions of Tundale; together with Metrical Moralizations and Other Fragments of Early Poetry, hitherto inedited."

For the sake of identification, it may be well to start this account[1] of Tundal's vision by quoting the opening lines of the poem:

> "Jhesu Cryst Lord off myghtis most
> Fader and Son and Holy Gost
> Grant hem alle thi blessyng
> That lystenyght me to my endyng."

---

[1] It may be of interest to have, for purposes of comparison, the sectional headings of the Latin text. Quoted from Schade's edition above mentioned, these are as follows:—

Visio cuiusdam militis Hyberniensis ad Ædificationem Conscripta.

1. De situ Hybernie primo.
2. De exitu anime.
3. De adventu angeli in occursum anime.
4. De prima pena homicidarum.
5. De pena homicidarum et insidiatorum.
6. De valle et pena superborum.
7. De auaris et pena eorum.
8. De pena furum et raptorum.
9. De pena glutonum et fornicancium.
10. De pena sub habitu et ordine religionis fornicancium vel quacumque condicione se coinquinancium.
11. De pena eorum qui cumulant pecuniam super pecuniam.
12. Descensus ad inferos.
13. De inferno inferiori.
14. De ipso principe tenebrarum.
15. De moderata pena non ualde malorum. [16.

and half a dozen lines more of introduction. Tundal is then introduced, a reprobate Irishman, and we get the date from this couplet:

> "A thousand and a hondryt here
> And nyn wyntur and fovrty."

The character and circumstances of the hero occupy quite a number of lines. He was "ryche enow of ryches," but "poore of all gudnesse." He was dissipated, proud, envious, and treacherous, a liar and a cheat, and in fact he is painted very black indeed, in order to heighten the effect of the *dénoûment*. His death occurred at a meal at the house of a man who owed him the price of three horses, and whom he had visited in order to collect the debt.

> "At the fyrst mossel so syttand
> He myghte not well lefte vp his hond
> He cryed lowde and changyt chere
> As he had felud dethe nere."

This is the least dramatic version of the incident. Delepierre's MS. attributes the seizure to a treacherous blow from his host with the axe which

---

16. De campo leticie et fonte uite et requie non ualde bonorum.
17. De Donato et Choncober regibus.
18. De rege Comarcho.
19. De gloria coniugalium.
20. De gloria martyrum et continencium.
21. De gloria monachorum et sanctimonialium.
22. De defensoribus et structoribus ecclesiarum et gloria eorum.
23. De gloria uirginum et ix ordinibus angelorum.
24. De sancto Rudano confessore.
25. De sancto Patricio et iiii notis episcopis.
26. De reditu anime ad corpus.

Tundal had just put off before sitting down, while Wright talks of an unseen hand as inflicting the stroke.[1] Be that as it may, the result in all three versions is the same.

> "From mydday of that wenusday
> Tyl the setturday after the none"

Tundal lay to all intents and purposes dead.

When his soul left his body it found itself alone in a dark place, weeping and lamenting its sins. Presently there comes upon it a troop of the most appalling demons. There are one or two descriptive touches here of a high order:

> "Her lyppis honget byneythe her chynne
> Her tethe wer long tho throtus wyde
> Her tongis honged owt full syde.
>
> . . . . . .
>
> Of hem cam the fowlest stynk
> That any erthyly mon myght thynk";

and so forth, "naylys" as sharp as ground steel, "hornes" and "taylys," altogether not a pretty picture. These fiendish creatures crowd round Tundal, and recognise him as a kindred spirit: as he has chosen his fellowship on earth, and been a friend of darkness there, so shall it be with him now. Suddenly Tundal sees a bright star in the distant darkness, which coming nearer proves to be his guardian angel; and by him he is rescued from the devils. He does not escape, however, without a reproof which is very much to the point. The

[1] This detail comes from some other source, but, in the main, Wright agrees with the MS. edited by Turnbull.

angel has been with Tundal from his birth, yet never till now has appeal been made to him, or his counsel been followed. He points out to Tundal the foulest and most ungodly of the fiends, and says:

> ". . . this is he
> That thou dyddst know and not me,
> After hym thou hast alway wroght
> But in me trystys thou ryght noght."

Tundal suffers in this department of Purgatory, but the pains are not particularised. His guardian angel saves him out of them, and the fiends blaspheme God's justice in thus letting a soul escape.

The pair then set out to see the pains of Purgatory, and arrive first at a deep dale or valley, the bottom of which is full of burning coals which throw off an obnoxious stench. On the coals is a sort of grid, and on the grid, melting and running through it, like wax through a cloth, only to be collected and subjected anew to the same process, are the souls of parricides and other murderers.

Next is a very high mountain, on one side full of fire and smoke that "stank of pyche and brymston," on the other a windy and stormy waste of ice and snow. The demons of the place are armed with pitchforks and tongs of glowing iron, and with these they hurl the sinners from fire to snow, and back again from ice to flames, in unceasing and agonising alternation.

> "This peyn is for thefus dyght
> And for hom that robry makis."

MEDIÆVAL LEGENDS

Tundal and his guide now see another valley, like the last flaming and smoking and stinking, only deeper. A bridge connects the mountains which form the sides of this valley, a thousand steps in length, and scarcely one foot wide. Tundal saw many souls attempt to cross, but none succeeded while he watched except "a prest that a palmer was." Thus are punished "prowd men and bostus." There are two bridges in the vision, of which this is the less important.

After a long and dark journey, Tundal comes to a portentous monster of ferocious aspect, described as a "hogy best":

> "In all his mowthe that was so wyde
> Nyne thowsand armyd in myght ryde."

Two giants hang between the monster's tusks, one of them head downwards, and a pillar on each side of its mouth supports its upper jaw, keeping the mouth open. Inside are three gates standing open and belching forth the usual smoke and stench. The attendant demons are engaged in driving the souls of the covetous into the terrific maw of the beast. Tundal is here deserted by his guardian angel, and endures a time of torment in the interior of the monster, gnawed by lions and dragons and serpents, and tortured by fire and ice in various ways. The beast is called "Akyron," (Acheron), and Wright[1] calls attention to this curious perversion of the classical legend.

Having got out, "he wyst not how," Tundal sees

[1] *Op. cit.*, p. 37.

the angel again, and the pair proceed to the next place of chastisement. This is a hideous and stormy lake full of "howgy bestys," which add their yells and cries to the din of the waves. Fire dropping from their mouths makes the water boil again.

> "Ouer that lake then saw thei lygge
> A wonder long narow brygge
> Too myle of leynthe that was semand
> And scarsly of the bred of a hand.
> Off scharpe pykys of yron and stell
> Hit was grevous for to fele,
> Ther myght non passe by that brygge thare
> But yeff her feet wer hyrt sare,
> The hydous bestys in that lake
> Drew nere the brygge her pray to take."

The attempt to cross the bridge is the Purgatory of thieves, who have robbed their fellows or the Church. Tundal sees a man upon it in wretched plight, his feet lacerated by the spikes and a sheaf of corn on his back. In reply to his inquiry, the angel informs him that the man had withheld, or stolen from the Church, his tithes, and so now "Therefor byes he hem full dere." Tundal had, it appeared, stolen a cow from a "gossyp," but had returned it later; therefore, though he must suffer on the bridge, his chastisement will be lighter. His adventures with the cow, especially when he meets the man with the sheaf of corn, may be imagined. His good angel again rescues Tundal from this predicament, and, as on a previous occasion, his touch restores the wounds which the punishment has left.

After this they come to a house made after the

pattern of a furnace, which pours forth "stynkyng lye" a distance of a thousand feet. Souls are being burned to nothing even outside this furnace, and when Tundal approaches near to the house where the furnace is, he sees "mony a fowle bocchere" standing in the fire, some terrible implement in the hand of each—a sickle, or a saw, or a scythe, it may be. The crime punished in the furnace is not mentioned in so many words, but there is some ground for supposing that it was impurity of some sort. Tundal is seized by the fiends, who "hewyd him in gobettis smale." Mention is made of a "hydous hond" in the house, which fills Tundal with "grette drede." He is constrained by the horrors of this department of Purgatory to question the verse "Misericordia Domini plena est terra," and thus draws upon himself another homily from his guardian angel, a rather crude and obvious exposition of the purpose of the purgatorial pains.

The reader is now introduced to another terrible monster, with two black wings on either side of his back, feet with nails of iron and steel, a long thin neck and a huge head, of which the principal feature was an iron-tipped snout. This creature sat in the middle of a great frozen lake, and swallowed souls. When these had been tormented by the fires and adders within the monster for a time, they were cast forth again into the ice; and so the changes went on. These tortured souls made such an outcry "that noyse of hem fell night to hell," and little wonder, for in the monster's stomach all sorts of reptiles have bred in their bodies and afterwards gnaw their way out. It is a hideous passage, and describes the chastisement that awaits those of the religious profession who have been guilty of impurity of life. The Jews are rather unfairly bracketed in the same condemnation, " Yf thei amend hom not or thei goo befor!" Tundal himself, though no churchman, has sins to expiate here, and he is accordingly thrust into the monster; for his condition after this experience let the text speak:

> "Seth thyn the best hym owt kest
> Then was he swollen as he wold brest,
> All full of edders then he was
> And non of hem myght from oder passe."

With no other light but that which radiates from his guardian angel, Tundalus now stumbles down a steep and narrow path. (The explanation of this is not quite satisfactory—"the way that lyght to the dedde," but the matter need not delay us.) This dark track leads the pair to a dungeon full of forges, at which stand fiendish smiths executing judgment upon the souls. This passage cannot fail to recall the transmigration process described by Thespesius.[1] The devils heat the souls in great fires, which they blow up with bellows, then lay them on anvils and belabour them with hammers. "Vlkane" is the name of the smith-in-chief, the second direct classical allusion of this MS. This torment also Tundalus has to undergo, the chastisement of "delytes and folys."

[1] Above, p. 73.

The angel now says that Tundal is to see yet greater pains than he has already witnessed, the eternal torments of the damned in hell. Accordingly they proceed on their way, and presently there smites them suddenly such a mighty cold that Tundal "was ner froson to dedde." To make matters worse, he is forsaken by his guardian and guide. Alone and in wretched terror he beholds a pit in the earth, spouting noisome flame, and a pillar rising out of it nearly to heaven. Round the pillar fly souls, like sparks of fire, and when they are burned to ashes they fall back again into the chasm. Hearing Tundal's groans and cries, the fiends of the pit hurry to him, and overwhelm him with threats and abuse. Their description almost excels that of the fiends of Purgatory. Amongst other terrifying details, they have tails like scorpions and nails like the flukes of an anchor on their knuckles. On the reappearance of the angel, however, the fiends scatter, and Tundal is led on to see the great enemy of mankind.

Reaching the gates of hell, he beholds another pit, or more probably merely another part of the same, and at the bottom of it, the arch-fiend.

> "So vgly was thut loghtly wyght
> Neuer ar was seyn so hydous a syght."

As for the pains of hell, if a man had a hundred heads, and in each head a hundred mouths, and in each mouth a hundred tongues, and if each tongue could speak with all the wisdom of all mankind, not even then could he describe them. Tundal then returns to the description of Satan, a pitchy black body of human shape and of enormous bulk. A hundred cubits was his length. When he gaped he swallowed a thousand souls at once.[1] He had a thousand hands, each with twenty fingers armed with sharp iron nails, and each finger was a hundred spans in length (a somewhat unusual proportion, it will be observed, to the total height mentioned!). His immense tail is armed with sharp hooks for the torture of the surrounding souls. And now appears a very curious feature of the story. Satan himself is lying on a grid over hot coals, which fiends blow into flame with bellows. He is, therefore, a mixture of the arch-enemy and the angel Lucifer, and the inference is confirmed by these lines, in which the angel explains Satan's identity:

> "He was the furst creature
> That God made after his fygure,
> Fro hevon throw pryd he fell adon
> Hydour in to this depe donion."

He crushes and breaks up handfuls of souls as he lies, and drops them into the fire, from which, however, as usual, they come out whole, to be put to fresh tortures. When Satan sighs in his pain, he breathes out a thousand souls at a time, and presently swallows them all again "with smoke of pycche and of brymston."[1]

Tundal is now done with hell, and congratulates himself on the mercy of Christ by which he will

[1] Cf. Alberic's monster, above, p. 221.

be able to escape the terrors he has witnessed. Before he reaches heaven, however, there is one more slight penance to see. Inside a fair round wall upon which he comes, he finds a class of people who have lived honest lives and are saved, but yet have to expiate a want of charity. They are in bright light, indeed, but naked. Amidst storms of bitter cold wind and rain they suffer hunger and thirst and " grett travell withowtynn rest."

Such, then, is Tundal's vision of Purgatory and Hell. He now passes into a land smiling with many-coloured flowers, from which comes a fragrance sweeter than tongue can tell. And there, without many more words, we must leave him. There is a good precedent for this course. Delepierre accompanies him no further, characterising his heaven as a weak effort compared to the earlier portions of the vision: " the details," he adds, " are mostly monotonous, and without imagination," and a perusal of them does not tempt one to gainsay this criticism. A glance at the Latin sectional headings above quoted shows at once the stuff of which Tundal's heaven is made. There are only five divisions which really concern the future abode of the blessed at all, or six, if the temporary abode of the " not very good " be included; these are full of martyrs and monks, virgins and angels, but of eschatological meaning they are practically void. Absolutely the only human virtues, by which is meant virtues of the everyday life of the layman, which are rewarded here are continence and faithfulness to the marriage vow. Tundal's heaven must be voted a failure, then, though he exhausts the whole vocabulary of praise in his descriptions of the brightness and glory of its various realms.[1]

Owain in St. Patrick's Purgatory.

The legends which centre round the Irish Lough Derg have given its name to the work by Thomas Wright, which has been so often mentioned, and, as may be expected, a very exhaustive and learned account of the group can be found there. The story of the descent into St. Patrick's cave by Owain Miles in the year 1153 was a very popular one, and deservedly so. Especially powerful is the infernal part of the vision, its Purgatory and Hell. It seems to gather up the threads we have been tracing through the centuries, and weave them into a design so masterful and so impressive that any further horror seems impossible and unnecessary.

[1] I may be allowed, perhaps, to quote one quaint passage of the Latin text which rather nicely describes the heavenly music. Tundal had a certain appreciation of the elements which make up the enjoyment of listening to a singer. The quotation is from section 21: "Omnia instrumenta nemine laborante sonos reddebant. Sed hanc omnem dulcedinem spirituum uoces superabant, quibus nullus erat labor in extensione uocum, non uidebantur nec labia mouere, nec manus ad instrumenta musica leuare curabant, et tamen ad libitum cuiusque melos resonabat. Firmamentum autem, quod super capita eorum erat, multum splendebat; dequo pendebant Cathene auri purissimi uirgultis intermixti argenteis pulcherrima uarietate contextis, de quibus ciphi et fiale, cimbala et tintinnabula, lilia et spherule pendebant auree. Inter quas multitudo maxima angelorum uersabantur uolancium et alas aureas habencium, qui leui uolatu inter cathenas suauissimum et dulcissimum audientibus reddebant sonum."

MEDIÆVAL LEGENDS

The vision was first written, as Wright implies, by Henry of Saltrey, in Latin, and was early described in French and English verse. The following version is that of Matthew Paris, the historian, who died in the year 1259. It is essentially a Purgatory legend, as the facts will show; the knight's descent was believed to constitute an effectual absolution.

Owain, one of Stephen's knights, obtained permission from his king to return to his native Ireland to visit his parents, and while there was seized with repentance for the wild life he had hitherto led. He resolved to undertake a penance "more heavy than all penances," to enter the cave of St. Patrick. This cave, the historian continues, had been shown by an angel of God to St. Patrick, who "was much exercised to reclaim from the dead the bestial people of that country, by terror of the torments of Hell and love of the joys of Paradise." The saving grace of the descent had been thus announced to the saint: "Whoever, truly repentant and constant in faith, shall enter this cave, in the space of one day and night he will be cleansed there from all the sins by which he has in his whole life offended God; and he who enters will not only see the torments of the wicked, but, if he continue steadfast in the love of God, will behold also the joys of the blessed."

Having obtained reluctant permission from the bishop, the knight betakes himself to the spot, and, under the guidance of the prior, performs certain preliminaries which are not important, but which perhaps recall Pausanias' account of similar ceremonies.[1] When the door is finally shut behind him, the soldier steps out through gradually increasing gloom, and arrives at a hall in a meadow or plain, of whose existence the prior had spoken. There he seated himself, and fifteen men presently appeared to him, of ecclesiastical appearance, newly shaven and clothed in white. These address to Owain words of encouragement and advice, especially warning him not on any account to turn back to the gate, which certain demons will assuredly invite him to do. He is to call on the name of Jesus Christ, and his release from any torment he may be in will thus certainly be effected.

Left alone, Owain "began to prepare himself for a new kind of warfare." Suddenly he hears the most terrific tumult round the house, "as if all the men in the world were roaring, and the animals and beasts," and presently the place is filled with hideous misshapen fiends, who begin to salute the soldier derisively. They undertake to restore him unhurt to the world above, if he will go, but he merely sits despising them, uttering never a word. At this the demons are enraged, and they light a huge fire in the hall and hurl Owain on to it, dragging him about in it with iron hooks. Bethinking him of the counsel he had received, however, he calls out "Jesu Christe, miserere mei," and at once the flames are extinguished. "And perceiving this the soldier was minded not to fear them any more, for he observed that they were conquered by invoking Christ's aid."

[1] ix. 39, 5-14, and cf. above, pp. 75, 77.

Leaving the hall, the demons now dragged Owain into a vast region where "the earth was black and the place was in gloom." A wailing "as of the people of the whole world" greeted his ears, and at last he arrived at an immeasurable plain crowded with the miserable souls of the wicked. They were of both sexes and every age, and all lay prone on the earth, face downwards, fixed through body and limbs with burning nails of iron to the ground. Dante cannot surpass the horror of this scene. "'Parce, parce, miserere, miserere,'" the souls cry in their anguish, "cum qui sui miseretur penitus non adesset." Meanwhile the fiends run about over the prostrate bodies, lashing them with cruel blows. They make an attempt to inflict upon Owain's own person the torments of the place, but he escapes, now and always in the like case, by calling on the name of Christ.

Another place is now visited which is similar but for two details. Here the damned lie on their backs, gnawed in various awful ways by the fiery teeth and fangs of flaming serpents. Vast toads sit on the breast of some, tearing with their "misshapen snouts" at their hearts. The demons, as before, ply their fiendish lash.

The third punishment of Purgatory which the knight saw recalls very forcibly a great many visions of which an account has already been given. Here there seemed to be more people than the whole world could contain, and they were hung up by hooks and chains of iron in sulphurous flames. Again, as of old, the idea of appropriateness plays its part in the scene. Some hang by the ears, others by the hands, the hair, the eyes, the head, the offending members being forced to assist in the penalty. Not even here is the chastisement complete without the lash of the demons.

Next the fiends conduct Owain to a terrible wheel, whose spokes and rim are covered with blazing hooks of iron. From these hang the wretched sinners while the wheel spins over a foul sulphurous fire which comes up out of the ground. The demons turn the wheel so quickly that it is impossible to distinguish the men upon it; it is merely a blur of fire. Others were being roasted by a fire, while the demons dropped liquid metal on to their bodies, or were being fried in frying-pans or burned in furnaces. Again, there were great cauldrons of melted pitch standing, in which the souls were more or less immersed, some entirely, some to the eyes, and so on.

The knight is now taken to the top of a lofty mountain, where he sees the souls crouching, looking towards the north, and waiting as if in fear of death. Presently comes a mighty wind and hurls the whole crowd, Owain in their midst, into a foul and cold river in quite another part of the mountain. When any soul attempted to rise out of the water, the fiends, running over the top of the river, pushed it back beneath the flood.

When Owain has climbed out on the farther bank, the demons show him a pit, belching forth filthy fire and stench, now rising, now falling. This, they say, is the mouth of hell, their abode,

MEDIÆVAL LEGENDS 245

and once more they renew to the soldier their offer of safe conduct back to the gate of Purgatory. When he refuses, they hurl him into hell, and he sinks down, down, amid the flames, forgetting in his agony his unfailing means of salvation. When he does think of invoking Christ's aid, he is blown back to the mouth of the pit by the force of the flames. There new demons greet him, who say that their companions have lied, and that the pit is not hell, which, they add, they will now show him.

These demons accordingly lead Owain to another river, foul and very wide, quite covered with sulphurous flames, and full of fiends, who tell him that hell is beneath its stream. Over this river stretches a bridge, impassable, as it seems to the knight, for three reasons. It is so slippery that one could get no foothold, so narrow that it would be impossible to stand or walk upon it, and so high above the river that no one could bear to look down from it without falling. The fiends urge Owain to attempt the crossing, and prophesy that the wind, whose effect he has already felt, will hurl him into the river, where he will be seized by their companions and thrust into the depths of hell. Nothing daunted, the knight set foot on the bridge, and with each step he took the way became broader. A curious line tells how the blasphemous outbursts of the fiends, maddened by his success, astonished him more than all his previous torments.

The soldier is now done with Purgatory, "unconquered and now free from the vexation of the unclean spirits," and, proceeding on his way, he comes to a high wall "of wonderful and priceless building," with a gate in it glittering with metal and precious stones. And first there met him as he went "an odour of such sweetness that his bodily strength revived and the torments he had suffered gave place to refreshment." As he drew near to the gate it opened, and emitted a gorgeous procession of all manner of ecclesiastical dignitaries from the highest to the lowest. Two archbishops took him in charge, and, blessing God and congratulating the soldier, showed him their country, which was the earthly paradise. Here was no night, but always a heavenly and ineffable splendour; but we need not perhaps linger over the details of the scene; they are already familiar.

The purgatorial theory which is expounded to Owain by his guides is worth quoting, though it is perfectly normal. Death is the penalty of Adam's sin, and though all the sons of Adam share a common heritage of original sin, yet in virtue of their baptismal faith they earn the right to return to that paradise from which Adam was expelled. It is the countless stains of sin contracted after baptism which must be cleansed by the pains of Purgatory. All the souls whom Owain has seen enduring those pains, except such as were below the mouth of the pit of hell, will one day reach the earthly paradise, and the duration of the purgatorial process can be shortened and mitigated by the masses and orisons of the Church or of the peculiar friends of each. Further, all the souls of the terrestrial paradise will one day pass into the heavenly paradise.

MEDIÆVAL LEGENDS

It is to obtain a distant view of this latter heaven that Owain is now conducted to the top of a steep hill. He looks around him and sees that the colour of the sky is as of "gold blazing in a furnace." The inhabitants of the earthly paradise are fed daily by God with heavenly food: "And with what manner of food we are fed," add the guides, "you will presently perceive by tasting it with us." No sooner were the words spoken than the marvel happened; for a ray of fire came down from heaven, and, spreading itself in points over the heads of all, seemed to sink down into their bodies. It was over in a moment of time, but Owain was so transported that he "scarcely knew whether he was living or dead."

It is unnecessary to prolong this account by accompanying the knight on his backward journey. The route, so far as it is indicated, is the same, and some of the same persons are seen. Of course we are not surprised to hear that Owain adopts the monastic life. He went to King Stephen and asked that for the future he might serve the King of all kings. The historian leaves him serving as interpreter in Ireland to an abbot with whom he is engaged in building a monastery.

A Cistercian Novice.

Wright[1] mentions this vision as one related by Vincent of Beauvais,[2] and though it is slight it seems worth quoting for its quaint idea in connec-

[1] *Op. cit.*, p. 39, note.
[2] *Speculum Historiale*, lib. xxix. cap. 6 *seq.*

tion with Adam; there are also one or two strong touches in hell. The year is 1160. The young monk has Raphael as cicerone, and visits paradise and hell. The former is the conventional city of gold, full of herbs and trees, singing birds, fountains, and streams. Above one very beautiful tree is a colossal man of great beauty, clothed with a garment of many colours from his feet to his breast. This is Adam, "pater humani generis protoplastus Adam per sanguinem Jesu Christi filii Dei redemptus." His clothing is the garment of glory of which the enemy of the human race robbed him. But from the time of Abel he has been gradually recovering this garment by the good deeds of his sons and daughters, and when he is completely clothed the number of the saints will be filled up, and the world will have an end.

After this they came to the "region of the shadow of death and a land of darkness." First are the infernal chimneys, through which the smoke and flame of the everlasting fire escape. This picture of the doom of self-indulgence is meritorious: "Post hæc vident hominem in ardente cathedra sedentem, ante quem stabant quasi pulchræ feminæ, quæ tenebant cereos ardentes quos impingebant in faciem eius, et in os, et retrahabant similiter ardentes per eius interanea, et semper hanc pœnam patiebatur. Hic homo, ait angelus, amicus fuit carni suæ, et inimicus animæ suæ, gulosus, et etiam luxuriosus. Cathedra enim signat, quod potens fuit in malitia, amavit mulieres, et ideo maligni spiritus in tali specie torquent eum." An even quainter fancy is expended upon the case of a thief and swindler in the vision; but one instance must suffice. Next occurs a rather remarkable passage. The novice sees bishops and priests and all manner of clerics, some laughing, some feasting, and others engaged in gluttony and dissipation: "quidam ridebant et cachinnabant, alii conviciabantur, alii studebant gulæ satiandæ, alii libidini explendæ." It is the comment which is worth attention. These pleasures themselves do not exist after death, but the torture of the sinners consists in acting representations of their past sins, to their great confusion and torment: "Non quod istæ voluptates post mortem sint, sed ad maiorem confusionem, et cruciationem similitudines peccatorum præteritorum in ipsis suis cruciatibus repræsentant, dæmonibus ad hæc eos cogentibus. Qui etiam postea eos percutiebant fustibus per media capita usque ad excussionem cerebrorum, et ejectionem oculorum, et hoc incessabiliter." The same idea is used, later, with terrific effect in the vision of Thurcill.[1] "Judas, the traitor," stretched on a wheel, and hurled to the bottom of hell amidst the blows and imprecations of the assembled demons and captive souls, closes the vision as far as it concerns the realms of the dead.

Bruno, a Chaplain of Magdeburg.

This vision,[2] together with scores of others, is told by Joannes Herolt in his extraordinary "Dis-

[1] See below, p. 262 *seq.*   [2] See Delepierre, *op. cit.*, p. 98 *seq.*

cipuli Promptuarium Exemplorum."[1] It is not a general vision of future pains and rewards, but a particular revelation of the fate of Udo, Archbishop of Magdeburg, where Bruno was a chaplain. There are no less than six separate visions in the section, which is headed, "De Udone Episcopo horribile exemplum," but that of Bruno alone is here relevant, and even it only to a limited extent. The archbishop was living in flagrant sin, scandalising his Church and town, and despised several supernatural warnings, amongst them an elaborate vision of a canon of his Church, who saw Udo undergoing judgment and decapitation in the cathedral, whither he had gone to pray for his superior's conversion or removal: "ut conditor omnium justus judex, aut citius morbidum caput Udonem Archi-Episcopum per interitum de medio tolleret, aut certe in melius commutaret." It was on the following day —the canon's vision was by night—that Bruno was riding on horseback, when, suddenly overcome by sleep, he dismounted, tethered his horse, and sat down by the roadside to rest. A cloud of unclean spirits surround him, bearing trumpets and drums and various weapons. They make a throne for one of their number who appears to be their head. Immediately another troop arrives, laughing and cackling, some going faster than eagles. "Room! room!" these latter cry, "here comes our prince Udo." The "satellites of Satan then" led

---

[1] This is part of Herolt's *Discipulus Redivivus*. The "Promptuarium" is alphabetical, and this story will be found under "Prælati." 8vo, Augustæ Vindelicorum, tom. ii. p. 782 (§ 516).

in the wretched soul of Udo in bodily guise, a flaming chain bound round his neck. Satan rose up and saluted him with ironical welcome: "bene venisti, princeps, autor et dilatator regni nostri. Ecce parati sumus tibi, et omnibus amicis nostris fidelibus pro meritis reddere talionem." And when Udo answered not a word, the arch-fiend went on: "Fatigatus est iste huc veniendo; et ideo placet nobis, ut consoletur: date ergo ei manducare"— "Our friend is tired with coming here, we command that he get every satisfaction: bring him something to eat." The demons proceed to thrust down the unwilling throat of the prelate a meal of serpents and frogs, washed down with a draught of liquid sulphur. In the same vein Udo is invited to the bath, which takes the shape of a pit of fire, from which, when the lid is removed, the flames leap to heaven and consume everything they touch—trees and mountains and stones, ay, even water—like straw. The demons take him, after the operation, like a lump of glowing metal, to their chief, who asks him with a smile if he has not enjoyed a delicious bath. Then, recognising that he is damned, the archbishop begins to curse Satan and all his crew, God, the earth, his parents, in fact "every creature in heaven and on earth." And the demons applaud and claim him as a worthy companion, since he knows their language ("canticum") and duties so well. For purposes of additional schooling, Udo is hurled to the depths of hell, to remain there "in secula seculorum." Bruno now has the misfortune to attract Satan's attention himself, and is on the point of being seized when he awakes in a terrible fright. He finds his horse very much agitated, so much so that it nearly tears his arms from their sockets before he can reduce it to quiet. On his arrival in the town, the chaplain finds that Udo has died at the time of his vision, which he narrates to his friends, urging his dislocated arm and suddenly whitened hair as a proof of his veracity: "ostendens etiam a sua junctura, seu compage brachium devulsum, et repentinam caniciem in augmentum veritatis."

A Monk of Evesham.

This story [1] and the one which follows, both told by Matthew Paris, are excellent examples of the Purgatory legend as it flourished about the year 1200. Both are elaborate and conscious literary works; there is nothing artless in either. They contain a thought-out scheme of penalty and reward, and are, as it were, merely incidentally in the vision form. The "Monk of Evesham" (which should be "Eynsham") saw his vision in the year 1196, and therefore, strictly speaking, Roger of Wendover, not Matthew Paris, is his historian. The English quotations which follow are from the translation of the former writer's *Flowers of History*, by Dr. J. A. Giles.[2]

The monk enters into considerable detail as to the circumstances of his ecstasy, but with these we

---
[1] Wright, *op. cit.*, p. 39 *seq*.
[2] Vol. ii. p. 148, (Bohn's Antiquarian Library).

are not concerned. It is perhaps worth notice, however, that he approaches the other world by "a smooth road, straight towards the east." The first place of punishment to which he is brought by his guide, St. Nicholas, is a marsh of hard mud, where all sorts and conditions of sinners of both sexes are undergoing torment. They are "bound in flocks according to the similarity of their crimes and professions." All are striving to work out their penalty and obtain admission into heaven, but for some this is impossible, for the worst sinners meet with a horrible death here, without proceeding farther. For the rest this is the mildest, least painful division of Purgatory. And the duration and severity of its pains is governed not only by the crime of each sinner, but by the good offices of living friends, and—a kindly touch—by the position and advantages they have enjoyed upon earth: "the less that they were in their former life supported by the privileges of honour, the more lenient were the punishments inflicted on them there." There is nothing new in the pains themselves. Burning and wounding with red-hot nails that pierce to the bone, demons armed with torches and forks, and so forth. All the souls here (presumably excepting those who pay the penalty of death) enjoy a hope of ultimate safety, and some of them consequently bear their sufferings with remarkable equanimity. The Latin runs thus: "Universi itaque ibi constituti, capessendæ salutis aliquando spem habebant. Quosdam vero graviora cernebam æquo animo perferre supplicia, et quasi de conscientia sibi repositæ mercedis, horrenda quæ perferebant tormenta, levia reputare."

The monk and his guide are wafted over a mountain, which almost reaches the clouds, into the second purgatory, which is a variant of the valley now so familiar to us, the valley of fire and ice. Here there is fœtid water ("fluvium an stagnum nescio") in the bottom of the valley, and the overhanging mountain belches fire, while the opposite promontory is the region of snow and hail. The spirits were " as numerous as bees at the time of swarming . . . their punishment in general was at one time to be dipped in the fœtid lake; at another, breaking forth from thence, they were devoured by the volumes of flame that met them, and at length, in fluctuating balls of fire, as if sparks from a furnace, were tossed on high, and fell to the bottom of the other bank; they were again restored to the whirlings of the winds, the cold of the snow, and the asperity of the hail; then, thrown forth from thence, and as if flying from the violence of the storms, they were again thrust back into the stench of the lake, and the burnings of the raging fire." Some are squeezed together so tightly in the flames that they remind the beholder of olives in a press ("quasi oleas in prælo"). Could Dante himself surpass this description in the same line? Such, then, being the nature of the punishment, there are certain features of it which must not be missed. First, it lasts, for each soul, until the whole surface of the lake has been passed through, though some manage this much quicker than others (just as in the first purgatory), according to the nature of their offences and the number of masses said by their friends. Again, the pain is far worse at the beginning, though not equally severe to all even there, and decreases gradually towards the end.

An interview with a goldsmith whom the monk recognises occupies the rest of this section. This man had been fraudulent in his business, and was now thrown into a heap of burning coins, which he had to count with scorched fingers, and even to swallow. This punishment, however, is not new to these pages, and need not detain us.

The third division of Purgatory is evidently intended to be the worst and most appalling of the three. "Little it is, I call God to witness," says the monk, "yea nothing, that I recollect of the punishments of that place." The scene is a deep-lying plain, "in demerso quodam terræ gremio situm," full of darkness and sulphurous smoke and stench, and covered with horrible and monstrous worms, "as the courtyards of houses are covered with rushes." Exhaling fire, these reptiles lacerate the souls, aided in their fiendish work by devils, who tear the souls limb from limb, melt them like metals, and restore them to undergo fresh torment. "Quarum vicissitudinum nullus erat finis; nec meta aliqua, nec terminus ullus." Piles of putrefying dead worms add their intolerable stench to the misery of the place. But this does not exhaust the woes of this Purgatory, for "all who were punished there had, in their life, been guilty of wickedness which is unmentionable by a Christian, or even by a heathen or a pagan." There is a further punishment, by another kind of horrible and fiery monster, in a manner appropriate to the crime. "Horreo referens et sceleris obscœnitate in memetipso supra modum confundor: dum mihi eatenus inauditum fuerat et inopinabile, utrumque sexum talibus immunditiis fuisse aliquatenus depravatum."

In this section also there is a colloquy with an individual soul, here that of a profligate lawyer who had died unconfessed. His story gives some further indication of the current belief as to the duration of the purgatorial pains. The lawyer fears he may not obtain relief even at the day of judgment, because his pains are gradually growing worse; and in answer to a question by the monk of the possibility of alleviation, St. Nicholas replies, "When the day of judgment arrives, then will be accomplished the will of Christ, for He alone knows the hearts of all, and then He will afford to all a just retribution."

The three visions which remain are of three divisions of heaven, or three states of the blessed, but the monk never reaches the "heaven of heavens, where the Lord of lords will appear in Sion," and though of course free from pain, these heavens therefore partake of the nature of purgatory. They are not very striking, and may be briefly disposed of. Speaking generally, they are characterised by the traditional splendour and brightness and fragrance of flowers, now so familiar. It is noticeable that they lie towards the inner regions of the other world, which in this vision, it will be remembered, is only located by the words "towards the east."

In what may, with the above reservation, be called the first heaven, the garments of the countless saints are thus described, "white indeed, but not shining; but there did not appear any blackness or stain in them, although they shone in an inferior degree of whiteness." The souls here have not been long released from the pains of Purgatory, and are waiting "in sure hope of the divine vision."

The next division is the "Upper Jerusalem," and its occupants have easily traversed Purgatory, "since they had been less ensnared by the vices of the world." Here an extraordinary scene is being enacted, namely, the Crucifixion, which crowds of grateful worshipping souls press forward to behold. The spirit of the drama is entirely peaceful and even joyous. "Near Him stood His mother, not anxious and sorrowful now, but rejoicing and looking with a most calm countenance on such an indescribable sight."

The third heaven is approached through an opening in a high wall of crystal, without end. A cross hangs in this opening, and, rising or falling, permits the souls who crowd round the entrance to go through, or, by debarring them, indicates that the hour of their passage has not yet arrived. Inside the door is a beautiful flight of steps, and at the top thereof, "sitting on a throne of glory, our Lord and Saviour in human form," amid a host of adoring souls but newly entered through the gate.

"But it was most evident to me," the monk proceeds, "that the place which I saw was not the heaven of heavens, where the Lord of lords will appear in Sion, as if He were in His majesty; but that from thence, after all difficulty and delay is removed, spirits ascend to that heaven which is blessed by the presence of the eternal Deity."

Thurcill.

Under the year 1206 Matthew Paris tells the story of Thurcill's vision,[1] and it is therefore covered, *mutatis mutandis*, by the same references as that of the monk of the preceding section. Thurcill's story is the most realistic, the most dramatic, the most fiendish, which is discussed in these pages. The hero was a small farmer of the village of "Tunsted, in the bishopric of London" ("perhaps Twinsted in Essex"), and his guide to the nether regions was St. Julian, "the entertainer." The direction of the journey is "to the middle of the world . . . towards the East" ("ad mundi medium (sicut ductor viri fatebatur) contra Orientem"). First, the pair come to a wonderful church, supported on only three pillars, the "congregation of spirits," where the souls of the newly dead are received and assigned each to his proper abode. The church has been specially designed, "through the intercession of the glorious Virgin Mary," to save the souls of the just from persecution at the hands of devils, and inside it Thurcill sees many

[1] See Wright, *op. cit.*, p. 41 *seq.*

of these just spirits, "white all over, and with the faces of youth." At the north side of the church, and attached to it, is a wall "not more than six feet high." On the far side of this wall Thurcill saw "a great number of spirits, standing near the wall, marked with black and white spots, some of whom had a greater show of white than black, and others the reverse; but those who were of a whiter colour remained nearer to the wall, and those who were farthest off had no appearance of whiteness about them, and appeared deformed in every part." It becomes hard to think that the farmer did not occupy his spare time by reading the classics.[1]

The mouth of hell is close by the wall, and the stinking smoke of it exhales "from the tithes unjustly detained, and the crops unjustly tithed." Thurcill's story has evidently been revised by an indigent cleric! The farmer himself was overpowered by the stench, and coughed twice—"and as those who stood round his body (which he had left lying on a bed at home) declared, his body at the same time coughed twice." We have already met with other instances of this "artistic verisimilitude." Of course the farmer's sensibility to the smell has betrayed him, and he is rebuked by St. Julian for his peculation.

The first division of Thurcill's Purgatory contains several of what may be called the prominent features of the mediæval scheme. The picture is drawn with a very Dantesque touch, and the

[1] See above, pp. 66, 67.

passage must be copiously quoted. The scene is laid between two walls which stretch eastwards from the church, and it consists of, first, a fire; this was not fed with wood, but "a sort of flame rising, like what is seen in a fiercely-heated oven, was diffused over the whole of that space, and consumed the black and spotted spirits for a shorter or a longer period, according to the degrees of their crimes." Secondly, a lake of water "incomparably salt and cold." "And the spirits which had got out of the fire descended into that cold salt lake at the command of the blessed Nicholas, who presided over that purgatory; and some of these were immersed over head, some up to the neck, some to the chest and arms, others up to the navel, some up to the knees, and others scarcely up to the hollow of their feet." Thirdly, and of peculiar interest, we have a bridge, "planted all over with thorns and stakes," which the sinners cross with varying ease or difficulty. The passage of those who had themselves been innocent of charitable deeds, and are now unassisted by masses, is thus forcibly described: they "walked painfully with naked feet amidst the sharp stakes and thorns which were set on the bridge; and when they were no longer able to endure the extreme agony of the pain, they placed their hands on the stakes to support themselves from falling, and their hands being directly pierced through, they, in the violence of their pain and suffering, rolled on their belly and all parts of their bodies upon the stakes, until by degrees they grovelled along to the further end of the bridge, dreadfully bloody, and pierced all over." The bridge leads to the "mount of joy," whereon stands a vast church, in which all the sorrows and pains of the crossing are soon forgotten. To this place also come the white souls, protected through Purgatory by a safe conduct given them by the archangel Michael and the Apostles Peter and Paul.

Returning to the church of St. Mary, the travellers are permitted to see further into the system by which the after-life of men is governed. They find in fact a judgment scene proceeding which at once carries the reader back some three thousand years to a very similar picture which has been described in these pages.[1] "The blessed Paul, too, sat inside the church at the end of the northern wall; and outside the wall, opposite to the apostle, sat the devil with his satellites; and a flame-vomiting aperture, which was the mouth of the pit of hell, burst out close to the feet of the devil. On the wall between the apostle and the devil was fixed a scale hanging on an equal balance, the middle part of which hung without in front of the devil; and the apostle had two weights, a greater and a lesser one, shining like gold, and the devil also had two, sooty and dark. Then the black spirits approached from all directions with great fear and trembling, one after the other, each to try in the scale the weight of their deeds, good or evil; for the aforesaid weights estimated the deeds of each of the spirits according

[1] See above, pp. 21–23, 25, 26.

to the good or evil they had done. When, therefore, the balance inclined itself towards the apostle, he took that spirit and brought it through the eastern door which was joined to the church, into the purifying fire, there to expiate its offences; but when the balance inclined and preponderated towards the devil, he and his satellites at once hurried away that spirit wailing and cursing the father and mother for having begot it to eternal torment, and, amidst great grinning, cast it into the deep and fiery furnace, which was at the feet of the devil who was weighing." Though not so convincing as the Egyptian method of weighing, this mode of judgment is impressive, and is alone enough to raise Thurcill above the level of his contemporaries.

There remains, however, that part of Thurcill's vision which makes it unique,[1] and a curious and powerful piece of imagination it is. The devils, it appears, have a specially constructed theatre in hell for their amusement, the actors and a portion of the audience being the souls of the damned. St. Julian and another saint, Dominius, smuggle Thurcill into this place to see the play. The seats in the theatre are constructed of white-hot iron hoops studded with glowing nails, and are filled by a multitude of souls "of divers conditions and sexes." The devils sit in a circle round the back of the auditorium, "grinning at each other over the tortures of the wretched beings, and recapitulating to them their former crimes."

[1] Though the idea has already been foreshadowed, above, p. 249.

The first to make sport for the fiends is a proud man, and he is compelled to strut and swagger on the stage amidst the applause and laughter of the watching crowd. Suddenly, however, his turn was over. " And whilst he was boasting about his dress, and was fastening gloves by sewing, his garments on a sudden were turned to fire, which consumed the entire body of the wretched being; lastly, the devils, glowing with anger, tore the wretch limb from limb with prongs and fiery iron hooks. But one of them put fat with pitch and other greasy substances in a glowing pan, and fried each limb as it was torn away with that boiling grease; and each time the devil sprinkled them with the grease, the limbs sent forth a hissing, like what is caused by pouring cold water on boiling blood; and after his limbs had been thus fried, they were joined together again, and that proud man returned to his former shape. Next, there approached to the wretched man the hammerers of hell, with hammers and three red-hot iron bars nailed together in triple order, and they then applied two bars at the back part of his body, to the right and the left, and cruelly drove the hot nails into him with their hammers; these two bars, beginning at his feet, were brought up his legs and thighs to his shoulders, and were then bent around his neck; the third bar, beginning at his middle, passed up his belly, and reached to the top of his head. After this wretch had been tortured for a length of time in the manner above described, he was mercilessly thrust back into his former seat, and when placed there, he was tormented in all parts by the burning nails [which stuck out to the length of five fingers[1]]; and after he had been thus taken from this place of punishment, he was placed in the abode which he had made for himself when living, to await further tortures."

In like manner are tortured a negligent priest, a soldier "who had spent his life in slaying harmless people, in tournaments, and robberies," a corrupt lawyer, and various other criminals. Space forbids the multiplication of details here; suffice it to say that the proud man's case has been presented at length not because it was the most vivid or appropriate, but because it came first. The picture of the lawyer's bribes turning hot in his pockets, and of his swallowing and vomiting the burning coins, is quite as forcible as anything that has been quoted. Slanderers are represented as gnawing the ends of a burning spear with lacerated mouths till they meet at its middle, and tear each other and stain their faces with blood.

Leaving the play, then, long before the curtain is rung down, let us follow Thurcill to more peaceful scenes. But first mention must be made of four courts of hell, each filled with cauldrons, where the souls of the damned are immersed for periods of a week in alternating agonies of heat and cold, salt and sulphurous stench.

---

[1] The translator's "and by having his five fingers stretched" can hardly be meant to be the English of the Latin text here used, which reads, "quinque digitorum in longitudinem protensis."

Presently, on Sunday morning, Thurcill proceeds with his guide to the church on the mount of joy, and there finds crowds of souls pressing round waiting for admission, and the more masses their friends say for them, the nearer do they attain to the church. They suffer no punishment here, "unless they were waiting for any special assistance from their friends." The further a soul climbs up the steps of the temple, the whiter its garments become, and inside the church were "many most beautiful mansions, in which dwelt the spirits of the just, whiter than snow, and whose faces and crowns glittered like golden light." These hear songs from heaven which refresh them "as if they were regaled with all kinds of dainty meats," but the music is inaudible to those outside.

Lastly, Thurcill is introduced into Paradise, a garden of herbs, flowers, and trees, all sweetly smelling; there is a fountain here, and it sends forth four streams of different colours. An enormous tree overhangs it, laden with fruits of all sorts. Adam reclines beneath the tree, a man of immense stature, smiling with one eye with "the joy which he feels in the glorification of his children who are to be saved," and weeping with the other for the judgment of the damned. Here follows an exact reproduction of a passage which has already been quoted from Vincent of Beauvais.[1] Adam is clothed up to the breast in a garment "of various colours and of wondrously beautiful texture." This is "the robe of immortality and the garment of

[1] See above, p. 248.

glory." Adam was deprived of it at his fall, but it began to be restored at the time of Abel, his righteous son; " and as the chosen ones shine forth in their different virtues, so this garment is dyed with its various colours; and when the number of his elect children shall be completed, then Adam will be entirely clothed in the robe of immortality and glory, and in this way the world will come to an end."

St. Christina.

After the elaborate creations with which we have been occupied, it seems hardly worth while to take any cognisance of this little story, which the Bollandists[1] assign to the year 1224. Labitte,[2] by the way, seems to have fallen into some curious error as to the date of the saint, whom he puts as early as the third century. In the *Acta Sanctorum* the story appears under the imposing title, " De Sancta Christina Mirabili Virgine, apud Trudonopolim in Belgio." Christina's revelation is simple and barren of detail, (these epithets would be ill-chosen for the rest of her story), but it includes an explicit threefold division—Purgatory, Hell, and Heaven.

Christina was a shepherdess, the youngest of three sisters, and died in her youth, " her body being weakened by the exercise of introspective contemplation." When her body was laid out in church, however, on a bier, and ready for burial, she suddenly rose and flitted like a bird to the rafters of the building. The congregation fled in

[1] July 24 (p. 651).   [2] *Op. cit.*, p. 713.

alarm, with the exception of Christina's eldest sister, and an elder of the church. One detail of the resurrection is not new to these pages: the "spiritus subtilitas" of the saint objected to the smell of human bodies.

Purgatory appears to the saint a dark and gloomy place full of the souls of men, amongst whom she recognises many of her acquaintances. The torments of the place are too awful for tongue to tell. Christina imagined that she was in Hell, but on inquiry she was informed that this was Purgatory, in which repentant sinners pay their penalties ("purgatorius locus, in quo pœnitentes peccatores in vita pœnas luunt").

In Hell, which she does not at all describe, are also some of Christina's acquaintances. In Paradise she beholds the throne of Divine Majesty. She saw the Lord, who congratulated her, and she rejoiced, thinking that she would always now stay with Him. But this is not to be; for Christ offers the saint a nobler alternative. She may, indeed, stay in Paradise, but if she returns to life, she may both rescue all the souls she has pitied in Purgatory, and turn other living souls to Christ besides. This she was to do by exhibiting in her own mortal body, but without damaging it, the penalties of an immortal soul; at the last she would return to Christ with great glory: ("peractisque omnibus ad me tandem multorum præmiorum mercede te cumulatam reverti.") St. Christina accordingly returns to the body, and undergoes before the eyes of men the pains of Purgatory.

There is an incident in the saint's life, apart from this vision, which is important to our subject. She attended a certain Luduicus, a count, at the hour of his death, and received from him a full and lengthy confession of sin. After the count's death she prayed that she might be allowed to share his purgatorial pain, and obtained her request: " His ita gestis videres Christinam multo post tempore nocturnis horis flammeis vaporibus [interdum vero frigorum algoribus] cruciari; et certum secundum quod anima comitis alternatis cruciatibus torquebatur." The idea of a living person sharing the pains of a tortured soul, and not in Purgatory, but simply wherever she happened to be,[1] is very curious.

After a considerable period of most miraculous and sometimes ludicrous sufferings, the saint dies for the second time, but even on this occasion the event is not final, and she returns for a few moments to gratify a friend. Then we read, " Tertio experta est mortem et tertia obiit, et sic transiit ad immortalia secula seculorum." Any one who knows the Bollandist Acts will surmise, correctly, that even now her miraculous career can hardly be said to be finished.

[1] See above, p. 225.

CHAPTER VII.

CONCLUSION.

PUT very briefly, the literary history of the Descensus Averno amounts to this. The visions began with simplicity and lack of elaboration, as we might expect, but were soon filled out and enlarged with more or less definite detail. By the time of Christ there are no less than three separate traditions, all of them substantial, which have grown up almost uninfluenced by one another. These may be called the Egyptian, the Classical, and the Hebrew. The reader will recollect how unlike Setme's story is the descent of Æneas to the shades, which may be allowed to represent the Classical tradition; and how different from both is, for example, the Revelation of Moses. It is not meant to assert that there are no points of resemblance, but it must be obvious that differences of soil and climate have produced three very divergent varieties of flower from an identically similar seed.

It was noticed, further, that at the beginning of the Christian era the "Visit to the Dead" underwent a necessary change. The Jewish vision becomes christianised, the Classical and Egyptian become a mere influence, betraying their presence by occasional touches. It was in the main the Hebrew tradition that lived on. From the first century two main streams of literature took their start, flowed separately for some six hundred years, and gradually mixing their waters combined to produce the fully developed traditional vision, as it is illustrated, for example, by the stories of Thurcill or Owain. By these two streams, which kept so strangely apart at first, are meant the apocryphal apocalypses on the one hand, and on the other those simple, pious legends in which the early saints and monks, who had not come under the influence of the elaborate schemes of the apocryphal writings, expressed their beliefs concerning the hereafter.

Through the whole course of this literature there runs, practically without exception, a consistent and singular characteristic. In every vision recorded in these pages the joys of heaven are pictured as spiritual, while the pains of hell are invariably physical. Purgatory may for the present be bracketed with hell, as for the most part it is a place of punishment; the chief exception to this being the earthly paradise, in one form or another, which it is fair to call the purgatory of the good, a sort of lower heaven. Punishment, then, is invariably physical; reward always spiritual. Why was this so? The supposition, which Delepierre[1] mentions only to dismiss, that the descriptions of infernal torment were figurative, is obviously absurd

[1] *L'Enfer*, p. 8.

and untenable. Was man not believed capable of feeling through his spiritual nature punishment sufficiently acute to meet the case of his crimes? This, too, is an impossible suggestion. It is a commonplace of all thought worthy of the name that the mind has more power to hurt than the body, that Remorse bites deeper than the serpent's tooth.

What is the reason, then, of this consistent materialism? In the first place, and obviously, the materialistic point of view is necessarily more popular. The physical treatment, and it alone, is dramatic and terrific, and doubtless served its purpose in its own day. Secondly, there is the very natural and easy connection of sin with the body; and, thirdly, that passion for appropriateness of penalty which has been shown to be so early and so lasting a feature of the literature of the subject. Not only what are commonly called fleshly sins, but a great many of the other crimes which we have seen punished in the various hells we have visited, are physical acts. The thief with his hands removed his neighbour's property. The moralist did not stop to analyse the motives of the thief, nor the warped mind and clouded soul to which alone such a crime was possible. "He stole with his hands" is the verdict; "by his hands therefore let him hang in hell fire."

It should be remembered also in this connection, that virtue was less positive in the early days of these legends than it is now, and the line between the good man and the sinner was drawn correspondingly lower in the moral scale. In pagan times, speaking roughly, the man who abstained from flagrant sin was a good man; in the Hebrew community, and still more in the Church of Rome, he would only need to add to his abstinence a priest's certificate of ceremonial fitness. Obviously, then, the question of personal religion goes for almost nothing; and all this tends to fill heaven at the cost of emptying hell. A hell which was managed on these principles would only contain the souls of sinners who might almost be called criminals, and a physical chastisement of such is, of course, less unsatisfactory.

It is only fair to say that this materialistic conception of hell, even in the comparatively limited literature of visions, (limited in comparison to the whole literature of eschatological thought), is not quite universal. Delepierre[1] mentions the facts which constitute the exceptions. He tells that Origen was condemned for holding the opinion that the fire of hell consisted as much in the stings of conscience as in material torment of the body. His reference to Bayle's Dictionary in this context produces the following interesting little story. A vision was vouchsafed to a certain good man who was in anxiety about the safety of Origen's soul, (a doubt, we may add, which he appears to have shared with many of his contemporaries). In answer to the fervent prayers of an old saint, this man saw hell opened before his eyes, and beheld the Heresiarchs, who were named to him one by

[1] *Op. cit.*, p. 8 *seq.*

CONCLUSION

one, and in their midst Origen "enveloped in horror and flames and confusion." This fragment is at least an indication of the unpopularity of Origen's views. Further, Delepierre observes that in 1215 A.D. the fourth Lateran Council condemned a certain Parisian theologian for teaching "that hell is not a special place, but that the man who exists in a state of deadly sin finds hell in his own self."[1] It is strange that the Persian poet should in nearly the same year have rendered himself liable to the same condemnation:

> "I sent my soul through the Invisible,
> Some letter of that After-life to spell:
> And by and by my soul returned to me,
> And answered, 'I myself am Heav'n and Hell.'"

By another coincidence, it is from the year of Dante's death that there comes a vision which possesses to a very marked degree the spiritual character which we have found wanting. Delepierre's reference is to the "Chronicles of Hirschau" by Trithemius,[2] and there is found one of the most interesting conceptions of the future life with which we have met. The vision occurred to a somewhat disreputable dyer named Godfried, who is described as "conversatione mundanus, verbis levis atque scurrilis." It is unnecessary to enter upon a detailed account of the vision, but enough must be said to show how very different it is from the main

---

[1] Delepierre gives the Latin: "qui docuit infernum non esse locum specialem, sed . . . eum qui in statu peccati mortalis versatur, in se ipso habere infernum."

[2] See under "Sigismundus Abbas XXXI."

body of such revelations. Godfried's sins, even his minutest thoughts, appear to accuse him, so open and manifest not only to him but to the innumerable surrounding angels, that he is overwhelmed with awful shame. This feature is already familiar from the vision related by St. Boniface in a letter to which reference has already been made. Words fail Godfried to repeat what the Judge and the angels and demons said to him. But still more significant is the passage where he directly states his theory: " Dispositio, qualitas, et modus pœnarum purgatorii et inferni multo sunt aliter quam a nostris prædicatoribus æstimantur." Later on, " Omnia quæ prædicatis in Ecclesia de gaudiis regni cælorum, vel etiam de pœnis inferni, comparata veritati, puerilia sunt et ludo puerorum similia." " The pains are spiritual," he says, " and I who have seen them and made trial of them in the spirit, cannot even explain in the body what they are." Again, " I neither saw, nor heard, but I understood." (" Neque vidi, neque audivi, sed intellexi.") " Nihil est ibi," he concludes, " carnale, nihil imaginarium, nihil sensui humano cognoscibile vel subjectum."

Those who are in hell are " sine spe, sine consolatione, sine ulla requie in æternum mæstissimæ"; while this is the characteristic of purgatory, " liberationis suæ spem certam in purgatorio habent omnes." Of the punishments of both places Godfried has nothing specific to say. Nothing could be further removed from the pitch and sulphur hells amongst which we have been moving. The punishments, he admits, varied: "sed tamen perturbatæ conscientiæ reatu, et obstinatione in malitia voluntaria cuncti fuerunt æquales." Again he says, "Pro demeritis anima ipsa propriis incendio ignis uritur, et pro dilatione fruitionis summi et incommutabilis boni ex desiderio cruciatur." Godfried mentions by name the vision of Tundal, only to include it with other similar conceptions in the following condemnation: "loqui per verba nota sensibus de futuræ rebus vitæ cognitis procul a veritate fit oratio remota."

There is something startlingly modern about this vision, with its absolute freedom from the materialistic traditions of its day. Sin is punished by Remorse, which is everlasting in hell, but relieved in purgatory by a certain hope. In addition to the stings of conscience, there is the torture of longing for the Good the soul now knows but cannot yet attain. There is no loftier forecast possible of the probabilities of Divine justice and mercy. It is a pleasing coincidence by which we are able to finish this survey at such a point. Godfried has struck a proper note, one that, even if it be not possible to agree with it, is nevertheless felt to give a worthy representation alike of the character of God and of the destiny of man.

Printed by
MORRISON & GIBB LIMITED
Edinburgh

T. and T. Clark's Publications.

HANDBOOKS FOR BIBLE CLASSES AND PRIVATE STUDENTS.

EDITED BY
Prof. MARCUS DODS, D.D., AND ALEXANDER WHYTE, D.D.

'I name specially the admirable Handbooks for Bible Classes issued by T. & T. Clark of Edinburgh. They are very cheap, and among them are some books unsurpassed in their kind.'—Dr. W. ROBERTSON NICOLL in *The British Weekly*.

COMMENTARIES—

Professor MARCUS DODS, D.D. **Genesis.** 2s.

JAMES MACGREGOR, D.D. **Exodus.** 2 Vols. 2s. each.

Principal DOUGLAS, D.D. **Joshua.** 1s. 6d. **Judges.** 1s. 3d.

Professor J. G. MURPHY, LL.D. **Chronicles.** 1s. 6d.

Professor MARCUS DODS, D.D. **Haggai, Zechariah, Malachi.** 2s.

Principal DOUGLAS, D.D. **Obadiah to Zephaniah.** 1s. 6d.

Principal T. M. LINDSAY, D.D. **Mark.** 2s. 6d.

Principal T. M. LINDSAY, D.D. **St. Luke.** 2 Vols. 3s. 3d. (Vol. I., 2s.; Vol. II., 1s. 3d.).

GEORGE REITH, D.D. **St. John.** 2 Vols. 2s. each.

Principal T. M. LINDSAY, D.D. **Acts.** 2 Vols. 1s. 6d. each.

Principal BROWN, D.D. **Romans.** 2s.

JAMES MACGREGOR, D.D. **Galatians.** 1s. 6d.

Professor J. S. CANDLISH, D.D. **Ephesians.** 1s. 6d.

Professor A. B. DAVIDSON, D.D. **Hebrews.** 2s. 6d.

Rev. J. P. LILLEY, D.D. **The Pastoral Epistles.** 2s. 6d.

GENERAL SUBJECTS—

Professor JAMES STALKER, D.D.
The Life of Christ. 1s. 6d.
The Life of St. Paul. 1s. 6d.
(*Large-type Editions*, 3s. 6d. *each.*)

ALEXANDER WHYTE, D.D.
The Shorter Catechism. 2s. 6d.

Professor J. S. CANDLISH, D.D.
The Christian Sacraments. 1s. 6d.
The Christian Doctrine of God. 1s. 6d.
The Work of the Holy Spirit. 1s. 6d.
The Biblical Doctrine of Sin. 1s. 6d.

NORMAN L. WALKER, D.D.
Scottish Church History. 1s. 6d.

Rev. W. D. THOMSON, M.A.
The Christian Miracles and the Conclusions of Science. 2s.

GEORGE SMITH, LL.D., F.R.G.S., C.I.E.
History of Christian Missions. 2s. 6d.

ARCHIBALD HENDERSON, D.D.
Palestine: Its Historical Geography. *With Maps.* 2s. 6d.

Principal T. M. LINDSAY, D.D.
The Reformation. 2s.

Rev. JOHN MACPHERSON, M.A.
The Sum of Saving Knowledge. 1s. 6d.
The Confession of Faith. 2s.
Presbyterianism. 1s. 6d.

Professor BINNIE, D.D.
The Church. 1s. 6d.

Professor T. B. KILPATRICK, D.D.
Butler's Three Sermons on Human Nature. 1s. 6d.

President HAMILTON, D.D.
History of the Irish Presbyterian Church. 2s.

Rev. W. SCRYMGEOUR, M.A.
Lessons on the Life of Christ. 2s. 6d.

A. TAYLOR INNES, M.A., Advocate.
Church and State. 3s.

Rev. J. FEATHER.
The Last of the Prophets—John the Baptist. 2s.

Rev. W. FAIRWEATHER, M.A.
From the Exile to the Advent. 2s.

Professor J. LAIDLAW, D.D.
Foundation Truths of Scripture as to Sin and Salvation. 1s. 6d.

Rev. L. A. MUIRHEAD, B.D.
The Times of Christ. 2s.

Rev. J. P. LILLEY, D.D.
The Principles of Protestantism. 2s. 6d.

Rev. J. STRACHAN, M.A.
Hebrew Ideals. 2s.

T. and T. Clark's Publications.

THE WORLD'S EPOCH-MAKERS.

A Series of Biographical Studies dealing with Prominent Epochs in Theology, Philosophy, and the History of Intellectual Development.

EDITED BY OLIPHANT SMEATON.

Each Volume contains on an average 250 pages, and is published at 3s. The Volumes will *not* appear in strict chronological sequence.

I. BUDDHA AND BUDDHISM. The First Bursting of the Fetters of Ignorance and Superstition. By ARTHUR LILLIE, London. [*Ready*.

II. SOCRATES. The Moral Awakening of the Western World. By Rev. J. T. FORBES, M.A., Glasgow. [*Shortly*.

III. PLATO. By Professor D. G. RITCHIE, M.A., University of St. Andrews. [*Ready*.

IV. MARCUS AURELIUS AND THE LATER STOICS. The Last and the Greatest Age of Stoicism. By F. W. BUSSELL, D.D., Vice-Principal of Brasenose College, Oxford. [*Shortly*.

V. ORIGEN AND GREEK PATRISTIC THEOLOGY. By Rev. W. FAIRWEATHER, M.A. [*Ready*.

VI. AUGUSTINE AND LATIN PATRISTIC THEOLOGY. By Rev. Professor B. B. WARFIELD, D.D., Princeton.

VII. MUHAMMAD AND HIS POWER. By P. DE LACY JOHNSTONE, M.A.(Oxon.). [*Ready*.

VIII. ANSELM AND HIS WORK. By Rev. A. C. WELCH, B.D. [*Ready*.

IX. FRANCIS AND DOMINIC AND THE MENDICANT ORDERS. By Rev. Professor J. HERKLESS, D.D., University of St. Andrews. [*Ready*.

X. SCOTUS ERIGENA AND HIS EPOCH. By R. LATTA, Ph.D., D.Sc., Professor of Moral Philosophy in the University of Aberdeen.

XI. WYCLIF AND THE LOLLARDS. By Rev. J. C. CARRICK, B.D.

XII. THE MEDICI AND THE ITALIAN RENAISSANCE. By OLIPHANT SMEATON, M.A., Edinburgh. [*Ready*.

[*Continued on next page.*

T. and T. Clark's Publications.

THE WORLD'S EPOCH-MAKERS—*continued*.

XIII. THE TWO BACONS AND EXPERIMENTAL SCIENCE. Showing how ROGER BACON prepared the way for FRANCIS BACON, LORD VERULAM. By Rev. W. J. COUPER, M.A.

XIV. SAVONAROLA. By Rev. G. M'HARDY, D.D. [*Ready*.

XV. LUTHER AND THE GERMAN REFORMATION. By Rev. Principal T. M. LINDSAY, D.D., U.F.C. College, Glasgow. [*Ready*.

XVI. CRANMER AND THE ENGLISH REFORMATION. By A. D. INNES, M.A.(Oxon.), London. [*Ready*.

XVII. CALVIN AND THE REFORMED THEOLOGY. By Rev. Principal SALMOND, D.D., U.F.C. College, Aberdeen.

XVIII. PASCAL AND THE PORT ROYALISTS. By Professor W. CLARK, LL.D., D.C.L., Trinity College, Toronto. [*Ready*.

XIX. DESCARTES, SPINOZA, AND THE NEW PHILOSOPHY. By Rev. Professor J. IVERACH, D.D., U.F.C. College, Aberdeen. [*Ready*.

XX. WILLIAM HERSCHEL AND HIS WORK. By JAMES SIME, M.A., F.R.S.E. [*Ready*.

XXI. WESLEY AND METHODISM. By F. J. SNELL, M.A.(Oxon.). [*Ready*.

XXII. LESSING AND THE NEW HUMANISM. Including Baumgarten and the Science of Æsthetics. By Rev. A. P. DAVIDSON, M.A.

XXIII. HUME AND HIS INFLUENCE ON PHILOSOPHY AND THEOLOGY. By Professor J. ORR, D.D., Glasgow. [*Ready*.

XXIV. ROUSSEAU AND NATURALISM IN LIFE AND THOUGHT. By Professor W. H. HUDSON, M.A., Leland Stanford Junior University, California. [*Ready*.

XXV. KANT AND HIS PHILOSOPHICAL REVOLUTION. By Professor R. M. WENLEY, D.Sc., Ph.D., University of Michigan.

XXVI. SCHLEIERMACHER AND THE REJUVENESCENCE OF THEOLOGY. By Professor A. MARTIN, D.D., New College, Edinburgh. [*Shortly*.

XXVII. HEGEL AND HEGELIANISM. By Professor R. MACKINTOSH, D.D., Lancashire Independent College, Manchester. [*Ready*.

XXVIII. NEWMAN AND HIS INFLUENCE. By C. SAROLEA, Ph.D., Litt. Doc., University of Edinburgh.

XXIX. EUCLID AND HIS SYSTEM. By THOMAS SMITH, D.D., LL.D. [*Ready*.

T. and T. Clark's Publications.

Just published, in post 8vo, Fourth Edition, Revised and Enlarged, price 6s.,

THE MIRACLES OF UNBELIEF.

BY THE

REV. FRANK BALLARD, M.A., B.Sc., LONDON.

CONTENTS.—Introductory—The Attitude of the Christian Church—Statement of the Case—The Realm of Physical Science—Facts of History and their Explanation—The Realm of Psychology—The Moral Realm—Christ: His Origin and Character—The Spiritual Realm—Complication, Culmination, Conclusion—Special Note on Haeckel's 'Riddle of the Universe'—Appendix—Index.

'From beginning to end of the book there is not a single dull passage, not a sentence obscure from overloading, not an argument skimped into shallowness, not a point ineffectively put. . . . The interest never flags; one is carried from point to point by perspicuous links of connection till all are welded together into a complete and rounded whole. . . . It is a perfect mine of quotation for men with little time for deep study, who are called, as modern ministers are, to be not only visitors and workers, but also preachers and teachers.'—*Guardian.*

'A most useful volume, thoroughly up to date, clear and telling in style and thought, and very well informed.'—*British Weekly.*

'By all odds the best apology of the Christian religion that has appeared for many a day.'—*Presbyterian and Reformed Review.*

'This is a well-written, reasonable, forcible piece of argument. We have been much impressed by Mr. Ballard's earnestness and acumen; his book is a real contribution to the large literature of Apologetics.'—*Christian World.*

Date Due

Library Bureau Cat. No. 1137